"*Overcoming Abuse God's Way*  n—how God's faithful lo ght up in the grip of abu sed her up to a new life. nd acceptance in all the give you hope and practical resources to live in freedom and love as God's beloved daughter."

—*Angela Thomas*, best-selling author and speaker

"Janet Marie Napper offers the reader a compelling and heartrending account of a life—her life—impacted by abuse and the long, difficult, and painful journey toward hope and healing in its aftermath. Written for a general audience, the book calls us to see the despair, the denial, the desire to escape, and the eventual determination that is required to change the stranglehold of the past and to chart a new direction. Survivors and those who walk alongside them will find her story a powerful lens through which to see the cruelty of childhood abuse as well as its long term consequences."

—*Nancy Nason-Clark*, professor at the University of New Brunswick, Canada; author of numerous books and articles, including *Beyond Abuse in the Christian Home* and *Refuge from Abuse: Healing and Hope for Abused Christian Women*

"When we feel that God could not possibly love us after the mistakes we've made, Janet Napper's story shows us that His love reaches as far as necessary to bring His children home. His all-sufficient love is the backbone of Janet's story."

—*Jack Branson*, author of *Terminal Justice,* coauthor of *Murder in Mayberry, Delayed Justice,* and stories of other cold-case investigations;

former US Treasury special agent; licensed private investigator

"Janet Napper is a living illustration of God's ability to make something beautiful from what Satan has tried to make unlovely. Anyone who has experienced abuse or abandonment will benefit from this story of a victorious woman whose power comes from her transformation through Jesus Christ."

—*Mary Branson*, author and coauthor of more than eighteen books, including Cutting Myself in Half and Murder i*n Mayberry*; president of AptWord, Inc.

After reading this book, I would like other teenagers to read it. It shows us how not to make wrong decisions in boys so we don't make mistakes and get hurt. This book shows you what to look for and not get tricked into being abused by boys and men.

—*DesiRaine* Age 13

"The beauty of this book lies in the willingness of the writer to be open and honest about her life. The format of each chapter (inspirational thought / what occurred / looking back) provides an easy reading path to follow. How fast you travel that path will depend upon whose circumstances you recognize within Janet's life story.

"You will slow down, ponder and even read again any section where you recognize a friend, cousin, mother, or even yourself. Has a long hidden secret been brought out of the closet? Are you strengthened to move toward solution? Maybe you are reading this to pass it on to another who needs to read this book and would not have known of its existence.

"I know that Janet is breathing easier because thoughts which had been withheld for years she has now chosen to share with others. The purpose for this book cannot be denied and can be fulfilled. Know that there is help out of the darkness of life. There is hope for tomorrow. You can move from 'Rags to Riches.'"

—*Joyce G. Kerce*, board member of Global GOGirl

"When meeting Janet Napper you can see in her eyes that God has already done a complete healing work in her life. The book, *Overcoming Abuse God's Way*, is just an extension of her life as an abused woman. The book is proof that through Jesus Christ there can be complete healing. This story of redemption and grace by our Father will sometimes leave you with a tear in your eye and sometimes lead you to kneel and pray for those who are in the process of experiencing their Damascus road as Janet did."

—*Joseph B. Raath*, executive producer / presenter: Radio Pulpit, South Africa

"*Overcoming Abuse God's Way: Rags to Riches* is a heart-rending story of a victim of abuse who has overcome, who is no longer a victim but a victor. Janet Marie is a victor! She has done ground-breaking work in South Africa to help women overcoming abuse, helping women to rediscover their worth and self-esteem and vision for their future through a community program called "Overcoming Abuse God's Way." She has truly inspired the women in South Africa, empowering them spiritually, establishing support groups in communities, training qualified facilitators to teach the program "Overcoming Abuse God's Way." Janet is also involved in safe houses for victims of abuse in South Africa where women and children of abuse are receiving the tangible love of God. Through trained women they will hear that they are valuable to God and He has good things in store for them.

"This book is a story of God's redeeming love. Giving hope to the reader. Like God did for Janet. God can take the mess of your life and turn it into a beautiful message. Thank you, Janet, for your hard, selfless work and dedication to the women in Africa. God bless you."

> —*Rina van der Berg*, founder of two shelters in South Africa, one for victims of domestic violence and one for neglected and abused children, many who are HIV positive. Rina represents the Northwest province at the National Shelter movement in South Africa which works very closely with their National Government.

OVERCOMING ABUSE GOD'S WAY

Rags to Riches

Janet Marie Napper
Brenda Branson

WestBow
PRESS
A DIVISION OF THOMAS NELSON

WestBow Press books may be ordered through booksellers or by contacting:

WestBow Press
A Division of Thomas Nelson
1663 Liberty Drive
Bloomington, IN 47403
www.westbowpress.com
1-(866) 928-1240

Because of the dynamic nature of the Internet, any web addresses or links contained in this book may have changed since publication and may no longer be valid. The views expressed in this work are solely those of the author and do not necessarily reflect the views of the publisher, and the publisher hereby disclaims any responsibility for them.

Any people depicted in stock imagery provided by Thinkstock are models, and such images are being used for illustrative purposes only.
Certain stock imagery © Thinkstock.

Cover Design by WR Designs, Wendy Reynolds
352-208-2941   www.wendyreynolds.net

ISBN: 978-1-4497-4929-3 (sc)
ISBN: 978-1-4497-4928-6 (hc)
ISBN: 978-1-4497-4930-9 (e)

Library of Congress Control Number: 2012907880

Printed in the United States of America

WestBow Press rev. date: 6/15/2012

Thank you, my heavenly Father, who saw me as a small abandoned child.

Who saw me lonely, desperate and fearfully hurt.

Who showed His love to me as a little girl.

Who saw my need and heart's burning desire to be loved by Him and others, and to love Him and others.

Who saw that glimmer of joy at the thought of serving Him, loving Him all the days of my life.

Who never rejected or tossed me aside when I rejected Him in my twenties. My heavenly Father waited patiently for my surrender to Him.

God is faithful. What He says is true, and that truth set me free— free from the grips of abuse while bringing healing and restoration to my spirit, soul, and family.

DEDICATION

This book is dedicated to my four beautiful children, **Peter, Christopher, Tara, and Richard,** who, through the effects of child abuse, never had the mother God intended for them to have. To my four beautiful children who through the years have given me joy and a reason to live, I love you with all my heart.

To **Jenny Van Buren**, the woman who raised me since I was two and a half years old. Mom, thank you so much for your sacrifice of taking me in while you were in your early twenties. Thank you for raising me as best you knew. I will see you in heaven.

To my sisters Carol, Bonnie, and Eva. I love you all so much and have been honored to be your sister. Without you, my life would have been unbearable and lonely.

To **Kenneth Jr. and Shelby**, thank you so much for sharing your father with me. I love him with all my heart. I pray God will bless us as a family for His glory and our well-being. I love you.

To my husband, **Kenneth Napper**, you are my miracle that makes my life complete. You are my best friend, my God-sent husband, father to our children, and "Pops" to our grandchildren. God knew you were the man to love me, to care for me, to sing me love songs in your gentle, kind way. The love of God in your heart draws me closer to Him, my first love. Thank you, thank you, thank you, baby, for praying for me daily, bringing us into His presence by worshiping Him in song and guitar, and for supporting Global GOGirl through your prayers, finances, and endless acts of kindness. I love you forever into eternity.

Thank you for our song:

Our love is unconditional, we knew it from the start,
I see it in your eyes, you can feel it from my heart.
From here-on-after let's stay the way we are right now
And share all the love and laughter that a lifetime will allow.

I cross my heart and promise to
Give all I've got to give to make all your dreams come true.
In all the world you'll never find a love as true as mine.

You'll always be the miracle that makes my life complete.
And as long as there's a breath in me I'll make yours just as sweet.
As we look into the future, it's as far as we can see,
So let's make each tomorrow be the best that it can be.

And if along the way we find a day it starts to storm,
You've got the promise of my love to keep you warm.
In all the world you'll never find a love as true as mine,
A love as true as mine.[1]

---

1   Steve Dorff and Eric Kaz, "I Cross My Heart," *Pure Country*, recorded by George Strait (Nashville: MCA Nashville, 1992), audio CD. Used by permission.

Acknowledgements

Republic of South Africa: A heartfelt thank you to the beautiful women of South Africa that took courage and went through the pilot program "Overcoming Abuse God's Way," especially Charmaine and Gugu. Because of that courage they came to the understanding of the cause and effects of abuse. Thank you to the dedicated ministry leaders from radio, magazine, and safe house directors that helped establish Global GOGirl South Africa and the Global GOGirl South African directors.

Patti Caldwell, thank you so much for believing in me, for helping me by your sacrifice with my yearlong mission to South Africa to help establish a home for abused women, where "Overcoming Abuse God's Way" was first used. Your unconditional love toward me is the first I have ever experienced in a person. I love and care for you deeply.

Susan Mahan, thank you for taking my manuscript and offering your help. Your contribution has made a world of difference as it moved with grace to completion. You are a treasured friend whom I greatly appreciate.

Wendy Reynolds, a heartfelt thank you for being involved in this project from the very beginning. You gently and lovingly encouraged me along the way with your time and artistic talent. Thank you for your loving character (patience) and the beautiful book cover you designed.

Brenda Branson, when God does something, He really shows off. I am honored and thankful to you for praying and seeking God with regard to contributing to my story. Your talent through the "Reflections" sections, mixed with my story of how God walked side by side as I sought Him to overcome abuse, made them my favorite parts of the book. You have truly captured the most important aspect of overcoming abuse God's way, which is to dwell in His presence. Thank you, Brenda!

Janet Marie Napper

ACKNOWLEDGEMENTS

Janet Napper, thank you for the opportunity to share in telling your beautiful story of redemption. It is a privilege to know you and a thrill to see what God is doing through your life.

Trevor, thanks for being the best son a mom could ever have. You are such a wonderful blessing to me. And I'm thankful for my new daughter-in-law, Brooke!

Angela Thomas, Todd Agnew, Brennan Manning, and others who were quoted in this book, thank you for your inspiration and encouragement. You are a bright light in this dark world.

Sarah Rebecca, thank you for the beautiful artwork. You are a blessing and a good friend!

Steve, thank you for being an incredible friend who has taught me so much about our Father's love. You are a beautiful treasure to me.

Jesus, my Lord and my God, thank you for every breath and the blessing of each new day. I love you. Thank you for loving me. Thank you that you take broken people like me and make them new by the power of your love.

Brenda Branson

Contents

TRIBUTE TO
CATHERINE CLARK KROEGER

This book is the fruit of much encouragement from Catherine Clark Kroeger, founder of PASCH (Peace and Safety in the Christian Home), Bible scholar, social activist, author, speaker, and so much more than words can define.

Catherine was planning to write the Foreword for this book, but unfortunately she died unexpectedly before the manuscript was complete. We miss her terribly.

It is amazing to recall the many ways Catherine encouraged us individually, even before we knew each other or began to collaborate on this book. When I (Janet) told Catherine about my work with the abused women of South Africa, she was very supportive. She provided books and resources for my trips overseas, and answers to my many questions while in that country. But it was Catherine's question to me that challenged my thinking and changed the course of my life and ministry. One day at our meeting, she asked me, "Why don't you start a ministry here in the US for abused women, like the one you're doing in South Africa?" Her prompting opened my heart and mind to ask God what He thought about it, and the result is what is now known as Global GOGirl.

Cathie has been a role model for me (Brenda) for many years because of her compassionate crusade to help hurting people and her amazing insight and scholarly knowledge of the Bible. She was a fierce defender of the faith and a prophetic voice sent to wake up the sleeping church. She was also an incredible encourager to me when I was going through a time of great suffering because of hurtful actions and inaction by individuals and organizations in the Christian community. Cathie stood by me, helped financially when I was destitute, and encouraged me to continue writing and ministering to others who are hurting.

Perhaps God used Cathie as the connection between Janet and me so we could collaborate together. We both want to honor her with this book. Thank you, God, for her beautiful life and everlasting legacy to this world.

FOREWORD

I met Janet Napper through a series of divinely appointed, fortunate events. The first contact was an e-mail asking if she could use some articles I had written that were posted on my website (*http://brokenpeople.org*) for her work with abused women in South Africa. I often receive requests like this, so I simply replied by granting her permission to use the material, filed the e-mail away, and did not expect to hear from her again.

Just before Janet left for South Africa, she sent another e-mail requesting copies of my book *Violence Among Us*, which she planned to distribute to pastors and workers in South Africa who were caring for abused women. I sent her a few copies and wished her well on her trip.

A few months later, Janet called me with details about her trip and expressed a desire to write a book about her life. Her dream was to distribute it to women in prison, as well as to women who were being abused here in the United States and in South Africa. She shared her vision for Global GOGirl with such excitement and passion that I offered to help her write her book and help get it published. Once again, I really did not expect too much since I'd made the same offer to others before who had not followed through.

This is where funny, unexplainable things began to happen. I began receiving text messages from Janet saying, "Kenneth and I prayed for you this morning" or "We're praying for you, Brenda." There were several text messages like this over the course of a few months. Now, I'm always glad to have people praying for me, but Janet did not really know me very well and could not have known that I was going through an extremely difficult situation during that time. One day, after my curiosity got the best of me, I e-mailed Janet to thank her for the many text messages and to ask exactly what she was praying for on my behalf. Janet's response cleared up the mystery. She intended the text messages to go to another "Brenda"— one of her friends who was in the hospital—but she "accidentally" chose my contact name on her cell phone. Janet and Kenneth may have been praying for their friend, Brenda, but I was the recipient of their text messages giving me the support I desperately needed at the time, even if it was from near strangers!

Over the course of several months, I began receiving "purse-dialed" phone calls from Janet. I could hear voices in the background, but no one actually answered the phone. Eventually, I called Janet and told her about the calls. We had a good laugh at the time but wondered what might be going on, if perhaps God was up to something.

The purse-dialed calls stopped, but Janet kept in touch by e-mail and sporadic phone calls. One day while I was in Memphis, Tennessee, having dinner with friends, I got a call from Janet, wanting to talk more about her book ideas. When I explained to her where I was, Janet got very excited because she lived a short distance from Memphis. We had never met in person, so she asked if we could get together while I was in town. I invited her to meet me at a Todd Agnew concert the next afternoon. Finally, after all the text messages meant for someone else and strange pocket-dialed calls, we met face-to-face. I immediately sensed Janet's passion for God and people. She is a dynamic, beautiful lady whose remarkable life tells the story of redemption and healing. Now I know what

God was up to when he orchestrated so many unexplainable events to make a connection between us so I could partner with Janet in telling her story.

As you read this book, I hope you will relate to some of Janet's struggles and be encouraged that no matter how broken your life has become, you will catch a vision of the beautiful story of love and redemption that God is writing for you.

INTRODUCTION

Abuse*: A destructive behavior that breaks down self, marriages, families, and relationships.*

Most of my life was all messed up, physically, emotionally, and mentally. The more I realized just how abnormal my life was, the more those thoughts played with my mind. The only way to cope with this loss was to make excuses and defend the very thing that kept me bound my entire life—dysfunction. Until I realized I could not do a thing with and for my life, I tried daily to scheme up ways to survive: looking for love in all the wrong places, pretending to be someone I wasn't, and manipulating to get what I needed.

People always believed in me, but I did not believe in myself; thus I took shortcuts. It is all I knew. I found out the hard way that taking all those shortcuts was the very thing that prohibited the fullness of my life. One of those shortcuts was denying Christ, believing it was easier and more fun my way. But only through God has my life been made right. All the instructions I will ever need for life are in the Bible. Being all God created me to be ... that is where riches and true contentment are.

Blessed is the man who finds wisdom, and the man who gets understanding. For the profit from it is better than the gain from silver, and its produce more than fine gold; she is more precious than rubies; and all the things you can desire are not to be compared with her. (Proverbs 3:13–15 MKJV)

The question most Christian leaders (such as my pastor, counselors, and women ministerial leaders around me) were asking themselves and each other was, "Will she make it?"

When I began to understand who I was (a person worth living for) and what I had (endless opportunities for growth and service), I began to live.

As you read this book, I pray you will receive *courage* to invite God to transform all the broken pieces of your life into a beautiful masterpiece. He did it for me; I know He will do the same for you.

Chapter 1

Left to Die

You have not lived one unloved day—ever!
—Max Lucado

THE STORY OF MY ABANDONMENT and abuse began when I was two and a half years old. I don't remember anything before that. I don't know what season it was or if the days were sunny and bright, but I clearly remember the lonely, dismal gray of our apartment in the city of Newark—dismal being the atmosphere of nothingness and gray being a feeling of gloominess and hopelessness.

It took three or four days for a neighbor to finally hear us crying. We were scared and all alone—just my sisters and I. My older sister was five, I was two and a half, and my younger sister was nine months old. Within an hour after the neighbors across the hall called the police, two Newark police officers arrived. When the officers opened the door to our apartment, they found three little girls left alone to die. My youngest sister Bonnie was suffering from rickets, a bone disease resulting from famine or starvation during the early stages of childhood. My older sister Carol had malnutrition. They found me huddled in a corner near the refrigerator, terrified.

We were taken to a holding facility where mothers of state-owned children could visit. These were mothers who had abandoned their children to be found by detectives or mothers whose children

1

had been taken away by the state for negligence. The hallway to our holding room, which seemed small and cramped with my two sisters and me, was long and narrow and led to a room with jail-like bars. Each time I heard the echo of footsteps in the empty hallway, I would look for my mom, thinking she had come for us. I had a combination of excitement and intense anticipation with feelings of deep loneliness, and an intuition that disappointment was just around the corner. As time went by in our small cell, the disappointment grew into desperate despair as I realized she wasn't coming for me.

The three of us became "property" of the foster care system while the police searched for our mother. When their efforts were exhausted, they began looking for our father. *Germaine* was the name of the man listed as my biological father on my birth certificate. He worked for the traveling carnival and traveled for up to a week at a time. This was one of those times.

None of our extended family wanted us either. I don't know if they just did not care or if there were other reasons why they could not take us in. While the State of New Jersey Board of Child Welfare searched for a home for us, Germaine's neighbor asked her sister-in-law, Jenny, if she would be interested in keeping three little girls who had been abandoned. Jenny was in her early twenties and lived with her husband, Pete. She agreed! I remember wondering who these people were and if I was going to move again. It felt good to be in a home environment with my two sisters and new temporary mother. A few weeks later, Jenny was informed by the State Board of Child Welfare that they could not find a foster home where my two sisters and I could all live together. They told her if she could not keep us, we would have to be put in separate foster homes. Because Jenny could not bear to see us split up and the state helped with our expenses, she agreed to let us stay with her. At this time, Jenny was told she could not have children and told me she had grown fond of us three little girls. We gave her a sense of purpose. The home environment at that time, best I can remember, was happy and fun. My two sisters and I had a clean home, clothes, and food.

To me, it seemed like my new foster mother treated us as if we were her own. She told me that when I first went to live with her, night after night I would lie in bed, shake my head, and say, "Santa Claus did not bring my dolly." For Christmas that year, Jenny bought me a doll. To this day, I remember that doll! It made such an impact on me, which was Jenny's intent. The doll was almost as tall as I was (about two feet), and she was beautiful.

Jenny told me that every day she would encourage my youngest sister, Bonnie, with rickets, to walk. She leaned her against the wall, held out her hands, and encouraged her to walk. Jenny loved us with everything she had, and we loved her.

At nine years old, I realized I was determined and feisty—full of life, curiosity, and attitude. On the outside I looked like a nice little girl, but on the inside I was confused, angry, mean, and deeply selfish. Sometimes I acted like a rascal, and I delighted in getting my sisters and me in trouble. Almost every night we were told, "I don't want to hear another peep from you girls, or you will get a spanking." Just as soon as the door closed, I just had to say "peep." Then, as promised, we all got a spanking and then went to sleep.

Perhaps some of this attitude was brought on by my sense of displacement. I knew I was different and did not belong to Jenny's family. With the loss of my parents, I felt as if I was living in a "paper house" which offered no stability or safety. The fear of being left alone again was always in the back of my mind. My foster parents argued a lot, which created more insecurity and fear that my paper house would collapse.

My two sisters and I shared one small bedroom. Although we

had the basic necessities of life—food, water, clothing, and shelter—I knew there had to be more. I always had a sense of wanting more, needing more. This realization at an early age eventually led me to hopelessness because I wondered, *If there is more to life, where is it? Am I not good enough?*

After living with our foster parents for a few months, Rosemarie, our natural mother, came to visit. Where she came from, what city or state she lived in, I had no idea. She was thin and pretty. Her favorite Disney character must have been Goofy because I remember her doodling his picture a lot while sitting at our kitchen table. Rosemarie came back once or twice more. Jenny offered her lunch, cookies, and a drink because she always appeared hungry.

Jenny told me after a few visits from our natural mom that she was going to adopt us. Rosemarie had offered to give us up for adoption if Jenny paid her ten thousand dollars. However, Jenny did not have the money, and my biological dad, Germaine, would not sign the paperwork. I don't know if Rosemarie was embarrassed or did not care, but she never came back. This left us in the custody of the state until we were eighteen years old.

At the time, I did not understand what was going on. Although I had a deep desire to get to know my mother, it would have brought even more pain and suffering to an already confused child who was trying to make sense of living with foster parents. I missed Rosemarie.

Jenny took good care of us as much as she was able. She received financial help from the state for each of us. Every year just before school started, we went shopping for new clothes and shoes. They may not have been the most fashionable, which made me uncomfortable, but they were new and clean. Being a foster child was never easy for me. Because of my parents' abandonment, I always felt worth less than other people—second fiddle or second class. The state's allotment for clothes was not much, and since image was everything to most young girls, I felt like I did not measure up.

Jenny was my hero because she rescued me from the streets and kept my sisters and me together. Even though she was kind and cared for our needs, she did not hug and kiss us or give us the verbal affirmation that I so desperately craved. On the weekends when we did not go to church, Jenny's husband took the whole family for nice drives in the country, surrounding states, military bases, and zoos. I cherish those memories of togetherness, even in the midst of deep, dark secrets. These outings provided a sense of belonging and brought comfort to my heart.

We had wonderful home-cooked meals, complete with salads and dessert—my favorite part. Christmas and Thanksgiving are some of my fondest memories. We would gather in the kitchen and help Jenny bake pies, prepare fresh turkey and dressing, and help put the delicious baked hams in the oven. Those are precious memories that I will never forget!

My real father, Germaine, came faithfully to visit us every Saturday—rain, snow, or shine—and he joined us every Christmas and most Thanksgiving and Easter holidays, which made my sisters and me very happy. We felt like we were important when our dad traveled to visit us every week. From what I remember, Germaine was a large man in stature, handsome, and appeared to be tenderhearted. He was a very hurt and lonely man who cried a lot, especially at Christmas. Although he never told us the reason for his tears, I believe he suffered from great losses in his life.

Germaine told us that Rosemarie was the love of his life. He was an alcoholic, unable to provide for her and his family financially, physically, emotionally, or spiritually. She looked to him for what he could not give and took her needs elsewhere. Frustrated with his own inabilities and inadequacies, he drank even more and eventually died. Rosemarie also had many insecurities from her past. She and her two younger sisters were placed in a Catholic orphanage at an early age because their mother, my grandmother, could not afford to take care of them after her husband was arrested for rape. Shortly after arriving at the orphanage, Rosemarie and one of her sisters ran away. When they were caught they were placed in a home for delinquent girls. Rosemarie may have had to bear some of the brunt of her husband's insecurities, but Germaine also had to endure hers. Abuse stole their relationship. Perhaps this realization was especially painful for Germaine during our holiday celebrations.

Reflections:

The loss of relationship with God, our creator, is the most painful of all losses. We were created to love God and to be loved intimately by Him. God intended for fathers and mothers to provide unconditional love and acceptance for their children, and teach them about His love. With this foundation, children will grow up as adults who develop healthy, loving relationships with God and others.

But when fathers and mothers do not know God's love and acceptance for themselves, they find it difficult to fill the love tanks of their children when their own love tanks are empty.

As an adult, I sought help from a therapist to work through some of my self-image issues. She began asking me questions about my childhood. As I looked back, I envisioned a little girl in dirty clothes, huddled near the refrigerator in a corner of the kitchen. The picture in my mind reminded me of an orphan child from a third world country in an advertisement from World Vision, an organization that feeds poor and orphaned children—a child with an expression of intense loneliness and extreme fear. When I realized this little girl was me, I wept uncontrollably. All those years of wondering if the stories I'd been told were true came crashing down on me. Was it really that bad? Had I been left to die, abandoned at two and a half years old with my two sisters? Yes, it was true! Yes, true.

My intense need to be loved began to make sense to me when I realized my childhood needs were not met by my birth parents. That brought more questions like, "Why didn't they love me? Am I unlovable? Is there something wrong with me? Will anyone ever love me? Am I too bad for even God to love me? What can I do to earn God's love?"

Another realization from my childhood is that I could not control my parents, my circumstances, or my world around me. I was powerless over them and my life. I could not control, manipulate, and play God in people's lives. I could not make someone love me.

Understanding this principle is the key for peace. But because I did not realize this for a long time, I desperately tried to control and manipulate people, events, and things. Unfortunately, it brought more pain and grief into my life.

Because these behavior patterns were destructive to me, I am compelled to warn you about the danger for your own life. You do not have to live unloved. No matter what you've done, and no matter what background you've come from, God calls you his "beloved" one. That's principle 1: *You are loved.* Stop everything you're doing right now and let that message go deep into your soul. Let this beautiful song of love drown out all the lies you've believed, all the lies you've been told. Listen carefully to the voice of love: "Arise, my love, my beautiful one, and come away, for behold, the winter is past; the rain is over and gone" (Song of Solomon 2:10–11 ESV).

Principle 2 is simple: *There is a God … you are not Him!* As soon as you release your grip on whatever or whomever you are trying to control in your life, you'll be able to unclench your fists and open your hands to receive all that God has for you. He is working for your good. When you really believe that, you'll find peace in the middle of your life storms and direction for the incredible life God had in mind for you before you were ever born.

Chapter Two

God, Why Doesn't Anyone Love Me?

The worst illness today is not leprosy or tuberculosis, but the sense of being unwanted, of not being loved, of being abandoned.
—Mother Teresa

Jenny loved us with everything she had, but it just wasn't enough for me. When I was a small child, abandoned and terrified, I lost my sense of security even though Jenny met all of my physical needs of food, shelter, and clothing. I always knew something was missing, which turned out to be the Father's love.

I wondered what it would be like to walk down the street with my dad. I would imagine talking to him about my fears and my dreams while he listened and assured me of his love. He would hold my hand tight and keep me from falling down. I'd hold my head high and feel so tall. With him by my side, I wasn't even afraid of the bully down the street.

I wondered what it would be like to snuggle in my dad's lap with my head resting on his shoulder. He would hug me close and kiss the

very tip of my nose while I chatted away, asking a million questions and listening to his wise and gentle answers.

When I looked into his eyes, I felt safe and loved. With my dad around, I would always have enough food, pretty clothes, and a place to call home. He was my hero, and I was his princess. My imaginary dad was someone special, and that made me special too!

My real father was a different story. Germaine could not provide the basic needs of life for his family because of his drinking and his work, which caused him to be away for days at a time, let alone the affirmation that I needed. He was a lost and lonely soul who was desperately hurting and struggling to find hope and purpose in life.

My foster father, Pete, Jenny's husband, was not the perfect father figure either. On Sundays, he took the family for a drive to many wonderful adventure-filled places. I remember loving the outdoors and scenic views of the places we went to. But there was a dark side to Pete. Sometimes he did crazy things, like dress up in Jenny's clothes, heels, and red lipstick when he was drunk, which embarrassed Jenny. This strange behavior happened when Jenny's close friends came over to play cards with her three or four times a month. I remember Pete and Jenny fighting a lot which made my two sisters and me scared. He yelled at Jenny, making her cry, and then he would find fault with us.

I was very hurt and surprised by all of this because for so long it seemed like our lives were normal, which to me was a home, two parents, food, and clean clothes. At that time, I was about seven years old. I really did not know when this fighting had started, but my sisters and I did not like it. I eventually blamed myself by thinking that if my two sisters and I had not been there, maybe they would not be arguing. Even though that was a lie in my mind, I believed it. The lies of guilt and shame, the lie that I had nothing and no one, and the lie that I would never amount to anything added heaviness to my hopeless existence. I believed the lie and became the lie. I was ashamed, I was nothing, I was hopeless.

Instead of being my dad's little princess, I was my foster father's little, dirty secret. The messages I received verbally and in action from my foster father's family told me constantly that I was ugly and dirty. Sometimes I overheard them talking to Jenny about me, and at other times Jenny told me what they said. However, even though I had been abandoned and left in rags to die until I was put in foster care with a man who was so vile, at the age of six or seven I had an inner sense of beauty and royalty. I did not know where it came from at the time, and it often got buried beneath the ugliness of my circumstances. In the eyes of my foster father and his family, I was a delinquent, a misfit, a liar, and other choice labels they gave me. People and friends in Pete's family judged me by the tragedy of my circumstances instead of showing compassion and sensing that I was trapped and needed help.

I do not remember who invited me or why I started going to church, but with all the family secrets and open family chaos present in my home, going to church on Sundays gave me a sense of belonging. As a ten-year-old child, I attended St. Mary's Catholic Church, where I first sensed a warm, loving presence near me, which I later recognized to be God, my heavenly Father. The nuns at St. Mary's were very nice to me, even though I did not understand very much about what was going on at church. Everyone at church seemed to be in unity and connected. It looked and seemed how a family should be. I felt a deep desire to be there all the time and learn more about God. I could not get enough of this accepting warmth that I learned to be the love of God. The peace I felt inside of me was heavenly. This unfamiliar beauty I was experiencing I had to have. This total experience caused me to pursue love the only way I knew how, by leaving several notes around the house, hoping Jenny would read them and give me a big hug, which would have assured me I was loved and accepted in "our" family. I had always been searching for a sense of belonging. The notes said, "God, why doesn't anybody love me?" Little did I know Jenny would not respond the way I'd hoped. She said, "You know I love you, Janet. Now stop leaving these silly notes." The embarrassment and rejection I felt from Jenny's response was very painful in my heart. My plan to get love failed and affirmed to me again that I was not worth loving.

One thing I knew for sure … I had a deep, deep desire to know more about this warm, caring presence which the nuns called God. I needed and wanted God, my Father, more than life. I decided that if I were a nun, I would have God's love and acceptance and His beautiful peace I experienced all the time. That was it. For the first time in my life, I had a purpose and a heartfelt dream. I was on my way to becoming a nun. I thought it was the only way to love God, to be near Him, and to have Him near me. I knew He loved me long before I even knew who He was. I was so excited! In my childlike heart I believed that finally I would belong to a family, the family of God, and He would be all mine!

I could not wait any longer to be a nun. That year I dressed up like a nun for Halloween. My foster mom cut holes in two sheets and put them around my head to drape on my shoulders, tied a rope around my waist, made a head piece out of some cardboard, and hung a cross around my neck. Away I went, pretending to be someone I wasn't and seeking affirmation from anyone while getting treats. I just could not wait to grow older so I could be close to God. I needed the love of God *now*!

 *Reflections:*

Jenny loved me with everything she had but it was not the love of God; therefore, I had no identity and I was never satisfied. How ironic for me to dress up as a nun for Halloween, walking the streets and parading as someone pure while begging for treats and affections from others. I did not realize my life would echo that childhood event—dressing up, pretending to be someone I wasn't, and begging for affirmation. I learned much later that God, our heavenly Father, provides us with *His* glory and *His* identity when we accept His invitation to join His family.

I believed that if you were a nun (or a Christian leader), you became holy and set apart, immune to human frailties and failures. I thought that life became a fairy tale with no more problems, no more need, no more pain, no more confusion, where everyone lived in a protective bubble, floating in emotions of pure joy. I did not realize that Christian leaders are just like everybody else—human beings who have needs and desires, hopes and dreams which must be submitted to God for His safekeeping and perfect timing.

During the childhood years, affirming words are crucial to our feelings of security and self-worth. We need to hear God's truth early in our formative years so we don't develop incorrect mindsets that come from the lies of others and from the father of lies, Satan, himself.

Because of the abusive language in my early years, I had no sense of self-worth. My identity was stolen as a young child but reclaimed later through my relationship with Jesus Christ.

Gossip and idle talk are like tasty truffles. The more we talk about one another, the more we want to hear; the more we hear, the more we want to devour. The more we talk, the more we believe. Did you ever hear the saying, "You are what you eat?" By consuming our talk, we start to believe what we hear if we feast on it long enough. That goes not only for the victims of abuse but also for the gossipers who develop the false identity of an abused child.

Little did I know that I am who God says I am: highly loved, blessed, chosen. I am not what Satan says to me personally and through other people. "There is no truth in him. When he [the devil] speaks a lie, he speaks of his own: for he is a liar, and the father of it" (John 8:44 AKJV). That is not to say we don't ever make mistakes or have shortcomings. Yes we do, and they often replay through our minds like a skip on a CD. Over and over we hear, "I'm not smart enough. I'm inadequate. I'm a screwup. I'll never be good enough."

In God's mercy, He sent me friends and people who were full of God's grace and able to see the value and beauty inside my heart. I was the one blinded to that truth because of the lies I believed and the abuse I lived in. I needed to take hold of the truth that I was loved *even if I did not see it*. I was beautiful in the sight of my creator *even if no one ever told me*. When I took my eyes off that counterfeit life and those deplorable lies and began gazing into the love of God, I began to see myself as the beloved daughter He created me to be.

But without knowing *who we are*—made in the image of a loving, kind, merciful God—or *what we have*—a purpose and hope—we will walk around in circles over and over and over again. You can go through life and die without knowing who you were created to be. It doesn't matter how old, how poor, how rich, or what color or shape you are, if you do not know your identity in God, you will continue doing the same things over and over again with the same tragic results, continuing to be hurt, confused, lonely, discontent, and seeking someone to love you.

God is faithful. He saw the heart's desire of a young girl who sensed His presence in a church and longed to experience Him more. Today I love God, my heavenly Father, as I did when I was a child. I am in His wonderful, loving presence every day. I stop to acknowledge and serve Him all throughout the day. He is beautiful and wonderful, and I am so blessed. I did not have to become a nun. He saw the heart and need of that young child and began His work in me. I did not make it easy for Him, though, as you will read later.

You are the Father's baby girl.
A daughter of the King.
Maybe you just skimmed over that powerful truth.
So take a minute. Close your eyes.
Take it in.

Daughter of the King.
Baby girl of God.

No matter what this world has been for us,
or the lies we have listened to and believed,
we must recenter ourselves on this foundational promise of
God.
We belong to Him.
Set apart. Claimed for all eternity.
Members of the royal family of God.
Daughters of the Sovereign.

And everyone knows the daughter of a King is called His
princess.[2]

---

2   Angela Thomas, *Do You Know Who I Am? And Other Brave Questions Women Ask* (New York: Howard Books, 2010).

Chapter Three

A Living Nightmare

Maybe you have known more than whispers.
Someone important has told you that you don't matter.
Someone who was supposed to love you violated you.
Someone you loved rejected you
with hateful words that you remember to this day.
Here is the most important thing I have learned
about that kind of awful relationship
or the people who wound you with their words—
those people don't speak for God.
—Angela Thomas

I DO NOT REMEMBER THE first time it happened ... when my foster father came into the bedroom I shared with my two sisters to touch me while he touched himself. It's difficult to describe what it means to be molested and violated. It's a crushing blow when your girlish, hopeful dreams of a protector and a provider are clawed away with every lustful, groping stroke.

Every night I was afraid. I began to sense he was coming like a smell in the air. My skin tingled long before his presence appeared in the dark—looking, leering, and finally lurching through the doorway.

Instead of receiving affirmation from my father figure, the message I received was that I was dirty and ugly. That message was repeated over and over again each time my foster father molested me. I did not realize it was proper to say no to him, and this betrayal of trust made it difficult to realize that I could and should say no to others as well. I felt different from everyone else and became very confused.

I became easy prey to other area molesters as well. The worst of the predators was the worker of a local convenient store, which I called the candy shop. I loved going to the store for my foster mother. It was my way of showing my love and gratitude to her, and my way of working for her acceptance and love. I went to the store a lot because she was a smoker and a lottery ticket hopeful. On one of my visits to the candy store, I was asked by the manager if I wanted candy. I said yes! He invited me to come behind the counter and get it. When I got behind the counter, he slipped his hand into my panties and fondled me. I was frozen with fear, and because of the violations from my foster father, I did not realize it was okay to say no.

There was a constant struggle in my mind. I did not like the touch of this strange person's hand, but I loved the attention. Because I wanted to please my mother, I did not want to say no when asked to go to the store; but I felt so ugly, so bad to desire the strange man's attention which came at the price of being fondled. The *fear* of telling anyone about this bewildering, frightening, dirty matter made the whole situation far worse.

Up the street lived some teenage boys who would watch me walking past them. I could feel their lurid eyes following me, wanting me. These boys were the neighborhood stalkers who came to my house, peered through our basement door to the kitchen, and then knocked on the door and asked for me. I was sure they were some of the peeping toms at my bedroom window in the dark of the night, watching me when my sisters were not around. I was so scared that they would come into my room to get me that I was in a constant state of alert.

Night after night, I'd lie in my bed in the dark, frozen with fear. The moon light streaming in through the window and reflecting off the lampshade on the dresser would look like the heads of the peeping toms. I was so afraid I literally wouldn't breathe! If those men, who were real in my head, heard me, what would they do to me? Terrified, I thought if they could hear me breathe, they would come in and hurt me. The fear was real. It felt like life or death, and I did not want to die.

In the early morning hours when I woke up, I lay there frozen in fear, plotting and planning in my head how to dash from my bed to my foster mother and gathering the courage to actually run. Jenny slept on the couch, so this was a safety zone; I wouldn't be near her husband. Jenny said she slept on the couch because of his snoring. I really don't know all the reasons why she slept on the couch. All I know is that I was glad to have a safe, secure place to run to in time of need.

I had no one I felt comfortable sharing this secret with. How could I tell anyone? I did not want people to think I was dirty or bad; I could not bear to have another label. They told me I was an abandoned orphan, a foster child, a delinquent, a burden to my family. I hated myself! I hated that I was fearful, shy, and weak, so I kept this living nightmare a secret.

To my knowledge, Jenny had no idea what was going on with my foster father because I did not have the courage to tell her. I did not know if she would believe me, and I did not want to hurt her because he was her husband—the man she loved. Only later in my forties did I tell my foster mother of those awful nights of abuse and fear. She said, "Why didn't you tell me, Janet? I would have put him in jail." Her constant love and support has been a source of security, strength, and comfort to me to this very day. But her comforting presence did nothing to alleviate my feelings of inadequacy.

Reflections:

The lie of abuse is that it is shameful. But in reality, the only thing shameful is the act of abuse administered by the abuser. Unfortunately, the one abused is often trained into believing they caused the abuse. This shame and fear prevented me from telling others about the abuse inflicted on me as a child.

The act of abuse administered by a father figure is truly devastating. As a young girl, I needed to know I was pretty and precious in the sight of my mentoring father and family, and thus able to understand I am loved by God and able to love others. I believe each and every person is created this way. Abused ladies need this concept underscored more than all other women. Innately, as a young girl I probably knew inside my heart that I was loved.

Fear controls. People who live in fear do not really live. Fear prevents you from making decisions and actions you would make if you were feeling self-confident, and contributes to problems in relationships and to various diseases.

Perhaps you have heard the saying, "Only when you bring a hidden secret into the light does it no longer have any hold on you." But if a thing is frozen, it doesn't move! Frozen in fear, we stay stationary and unable to move forward or backward. Therefore, the abuse that we have suffered stays hidden and keeps us in prison. *Tell someone* if you have been abused!

If even for a moment you could grasp how outrageously you are loved by God, it would change everything. It would change how you see yourself in the mirror: not better, not worse, *just loved*. It would change what you give to others: not justice or vengeance, but mercy. It would change how you live: no regrets, no pride, just gratitude.[3]

When God bends down in His mercy
and forgives a helpless, little, beat-up woman like you or me,
then no matter what anyone says
or how many voices you hear in your head,
or how long it takes you to believe it,
you have been made clean.
You are forgiven.
It's time to hold your head up.[4]

---

3   Adapted from a quote by Sheila Walsh.

4   Angela Thomas, *When Wallflowers Dance: Becoming a Woman of Righteous Confidence* (Nashville: Thomas Nelson, 2007).

Chapter Four

Searching

Today you are God's treasure. The only part of
creation he breathed to life.
Don't let someone define you differently.
—Jonathan Acuff

WHEN I APPROACHED MY JUNIOR high school years, I continued looking for worth and value, but in all the wrong places. In my quest for love, I gave in to the advances of neighborhood men, boys, and peers because I was afraid to say no.

It became harder and harder to concentrate on my school work. When I read a paragraph from a text book, trying so hard to focus and retain something, it became discouraging to get to the end of the passage and not remember anything I had just read. But no matter how hard I tried, my grades were mostly Cs and sometimes even Fs.

This confirmed the lies in my head that I was worthless. The messages from my foster father and his side of the family continued to shred every ounce of self-esteem when they reminded me that I was an orphan, a foster child, a delinquent, and a burden to my family. They told me I was ugly, bad, and useless, and I would never amount to anything. I believed them.

When I was sad, they accused me of being angry, so I hid my

true feelings behind a fake smile. My life was broken, and my heart was desperately sad and lonely. I knew of no other way to cope or survive except by hiding the real hurting me.

As a young teenager, I wanted acceptance from my peers, which I did not have from my family. I started drinking, smoking cigarettes and marijuana, taking speed, and having sex to cope with the pain and emptiness inside. I knew in my heart it was wrong, but I needed to belong. I told myself I was one of them and that they respected and cared about me; but in my heart, I knew I was simply a follower, not anyone of importance. Even Germaine, my biological father, dropped a bombshell when I was thirteen, saying "I'm not really your father."

Following the crowd left me feeling very ashamed and ugly. My dream of becoming a nun was definitely shattered because nuns are supposed to be virgins. By the end of my thirteenth birthday, I was no longer a virgin. I thought I would never be good enough for God anymore.

Sex, drugs, and alcohol put my life on hold. My world was lonely and fake, but I knew no other way to exist. I was deceived into thinking God would no longer want me, so in my mind I left Him, although my spirit still yearned for Him.

I continued searching for something, anything, anyone to fill that gaping hole in my heart, looking everywhere for worth and acceptance.

Reflections:

Because I felt so guilty about my behavior, I thought God was disappointed in me. I was scared He would just give up on me like everyone else had, and would eventually leave me. But the truth is ... God was *never* disappointed in me! And He is not disappointed in you either. Why? Because He knows us inside and out, He knows our thoughts even before we think them, and He knows what we will do even before we take a step or make a plan. Here's the best part: *And He loves us anyway!* So there is nothing we can ever do to disappoint Him because nothing catches Him by surprise. He knows us intimately, and His compassion toward us is limitless.

How different my life would have been if I had known this truth as a teenager, but thankfully God sent people and friends into my life who recognized the beauty and treasure behind the mask I was still wearing. They helped me see myself as someone beloved and cherished by God, as someone beautiful in the sight of my Creator, even if I did not see it.

Do you have trouble believing you are beautiful? Do you wonder if your mistakes are too big for God to forgive? Do you feel more guilt than acceptance? Do you feel perpetually stuck in the role of a victim? You're not alone. But there is a way to get a different perspective, if you're willing to risk it!

Are you ready? Here's the secret ... it has to do with where you look, the direction in which your eyes are focused. If you look at yourself, at your circumstances, and at the people who have caused your pain, the picture can be pretty grim. But if you lift your eyes upward a bit, past yourself and your feelings of guilt and shame, past those who have hurt you, and past those who have unfairly judged you, you'll see the smiling face of your true Father, the only Father, who knows how to love you perfectly and completely.

If you're afraid to look up because you might see anger in His eyes, then you've been listening to the lies of the enemy who wants you to be afraid. Go ahead, look up, move closer, and you'll see such tenderness and love that it will take your breath away. Why would God look at you that way? Because He sees the beautiful person inside who was created in His image, who often hides behind a mask to please other people and to keep from being hurt again. He sees the real you, and as a proud Father, His arms are open wide, cheering for you to take your first step toward Him.

Don't look away! Now open your ears and listen to the songs He is singing over you (Zephaniah 3:17)—songs of acceptance and gladness. Did you hear it? *You are accepted!* Let that sink in ... the longing for acceptance, the need for approval, all the things you've done to gain what you already have!

You see, acceptance from God is not based on anything you can achieve, and it is not lost by anything you can ever do. It does not come *from* you—it is His gift *to* you. This gift was wrapped up in a baby who was born in Bethlehem, named Jesus. He came to do something for you that you could never do for yourself—make a way for you to be accepted and approved by God. He did it! You've been forgiven, now you need to repent—stop being self-reliant, turn around, and go in His direction—and trust that what He says is true. You've already been invited to the party ... all you need to do is accept the invitation and come. God even provides the party dress!

Maybe it's time for you to stop striving, refocus your gaze, and rest in what He has already done. Shhh ... listen! Can you hear it?

I've been waiting to dance with you in fields full of colors you've never seen.

I've been waiting to show you beauty you never dreamed that's always been in you.

I've been waiting to see you tremble as you're embraced by a world saturated by my love.

I've been waiting for the day when at last I get to say, "My child, you are finally home."[5]

The Lord your God is in your midst, a mighty one who will save; he will rejoice over you with gladness; he will quiet you by his love; he will exult over you with loud singing.
(Zephaniah 3:17 ESV)

---

5   Todd Agnew, "Martyr's Song," *Better Questions* (Memphis: Ardent Records, 2007), audio CD.

Chapter 5

Easy Prey!

Sexuality is a soul issue that finds its expression in the body.
When it remains only in the body, or when the body
is merely used for sexual purposes, there is no real
connection, and the soul comes out the loser.
—Nicole Johnson

DURING MY HIGH SCHOOL YEARS, I was so discouraged because it was difficult for me to concentrate on my studies. I felt like I just did not have what it took to make it in school. So I began to focus on my appearance, clothes, and makeup; and instead of studying my textbooks, I studied boys. They were fascinating to me, possibly because I did not have any brothers. I read anything I could get my hands on to gain an understanding of boys—how they thought and what made them tick.

Boys and men were constantly in pursuit of me. As I walked to and from school, men would beep their car horns, circle the block, try to convince me to get into their car, and offer me money for sex. Many of the boys in high school (and some girls as well) were aggressive in their attempts to have sex with me.

In 1974, just days before school ended, a guy friend asked if I wanted to go smoking with him right down the road. He was pretty cool, and I was happy that he noticed me, so I said yes. He suggested we cut through the local junkyard and hang out there. We stopped near a large, dirty junk car, and he forced me into it. When he insisted I take off my clothes for sex, I had to think quickly. I did not want to do it! I was such an experienced victim at this point that I thought if I could fake him out, I would have a chance of running for my life! I started taking off my blouse and insisted he take off his pants, telling him it wasn't fair for me to be the only one to take off my clothes. Oh, the look of surprise and joy on his face! He almost fell over in his haste while he began dropping his pants.

When his pants were down to his ankles, I ran as fast as I could, quickly putting on my blouse and buttoning it up as I ran to the street. I stopped in front of a moving car and begged for a ride. The driver looked helpless and distraught, as I was sobbing uncontrollably, but he said, "Get in." He drove me to my house where my foster mother called the police. But since my friend knew the police, like most of the other guys in that town, he got away with it. I was made to look like a liar.

During the summer of 1974, after my near-rape experience, a girlfriend invited me to the beach. It was an extremely boring summer, and I begged my foster mother to let me go. I was thrilled that I finally had an invitation to do something! I loved going to the beach and enjoyed the smell of the salted sea, the sound of the blowing wind, and the sense of endless space. At the beach, I felt safe and happy.

My girlfriend said her boyfriend's friend was there waiting for them and he did not have a date. She thought we could meet. Anxious to get out of the house for the weekend, I agreed When we arrived, I saw this tall, thin, blonde guy who had huge green eyes. He appeared to be very shy and polite. I was happy and thought everything would be okay.

Unfortunately, like most guys in my life up until that time, he wanted to have sex that evening. I was too afraid to say no. It was humiliating to share the same room with my girlfriend and her boyfriend, especially while we were having sex in the bed next to theirs. For the sake of surviving, I pretended everything was okay, but I hated to go to bed the second night because I knew it was going to happen again.

The weekend was over, and although at times it was fun, it was mentally traumatic. I felt so ashamed. At sixteen, the one question I asked over and over was, "Why does everyone want sex from me?" I was afraid to take a stand for myself and afraid to say no. Because I felt rejected by both of my father figures, I sought that affirmation, acceptance, and love from others. This made me "easy prey."

Reflections:

Now I know the answer to the question "Why does every one want sex from me?" It was because I appeared to be "easy," when in reality I was just afraid to take a stand for myself, afraid to say no, and had a desperate need to be loved.

I needed to be loved and accepted, and did not realize that the way a girl dresses or walks and talks sends a message that she will do whatever it takes to find love in order to survive more pain and loneliness. I did not know I was already loved and accepted by God, so I continued seeking a counterfeit substitute.

The desire to be loved and accepted is a God-given desire. Our longing for relationship is designed by God but grossly distorted by Satan. God offers a selfless, sacrificial love that *gives* everything for the good of another person, but Satan offers a lustful grasping that *takes* everything and gives nothing.

We are designed to desire the attention and protection of God, our perfect Father, who loves us with tenderness and affirms us with kindness—a Father we can trust completely. But Satan has corrupted the hearts of many earthly fathers who abuse their children and break their spirits.

God created us as spiritual beings in a physical body that is intelligent, sexual, and emotional—gendered image bearers of His glory. He designed sexual intimacy in marriage as a beautiful picture of the love, unity, and "oneness" that exists within the trinity of the Father, Son, and Holy Spirit. But Satan, the great counterfeiter, has deceived us by masquerading sex as love and substituting casual "hooking up" for relationship and intimacy.

Here is the lesson I've learned about love. Real love waits and is respectful. Lust seeks immediate gratification and is disrespectful. Love gives, but lust takes.

If you're involved in a relationship where you are being pressured to have sex outside of marriage, then you are being disrespected and used. You are being lusted after but not loved. Maybe you've given yourself to someone who has betrayed your trust and abused your body. You may have given up the search for someone to love the real you, and you've settled for anyone who will give you just a moment or two of counterfeit love. Maybe your heart has been so wounded that you've built walls of protection that won't allow anyone to hurt you ever again.

If that sounds like you, I have good news. God knows the real you—the woman inside who yearns to be known and loved … and accepted. He knows you intimately and still loves you with a never-ending, lavish love. He knows everything you've done, all the times you've traded love for sex, and yet He cherishes you and desires to show you what real love is all about.

"The woman who belongs to God gets to dance. Inside the strength of His embrace, you can become the woman you have always wanted to be … the one He dreamed of when He dreamed of you. Your Creator has amazing plans that still lie in front of you. No matter what has come to you, the disappointments you have known, the consequences you have received, or the wounds that have kept you down. Even if you have truly failed or wasted a lot of precious time, it is never too late to dance with God! Jesus said, I came to give life—life in all its fullness (John 10:10 NCV), and no woman who makes her life in Christ has to live empty."[6]

---

6   Angela Thomas, *When Wallflowers Dance: Becoming a Woman of Righteous Confidence* (Nashville: Thomas Nelson, 2007).

Chapter 6

Twisted Love

*While the desire for love has seldom been so directly
expressed, love in its daily appearance has seldom
looked so broken.*
—*Henri Nouwen*

A COUPLE OF DAYS AFTER my weekend fling, the guy I met at the beach called to ask me on a date. I enjoyed the attention and closeness, but felt guilty about being sexually intimate. I felt sorry for him because he looked "needy." Within a couple of months, at age sixteen, I became pregnant with my first child.

I had very mixed emotions. The thought of having a baby terrified me. I could not take care of myself, much less a little baby. I had dreams of going out with my friends and forgetting I had a child to take care of. But the thought of having a baby also excited me and gave me a sense of purpose. It would be something of my very own to nurture. I was so confused.

I tried to hide my pregnancy from my family and people around me. I was afraid of what Jenny would do and say. I just could not handle rejection from another parent. I needed every bit of love and support I could get.

My body did not show the pregnancy until I was in my fifth month. By this time, I had gone to Planned Parenthood twice: the first time was three months after not having a period and the second time was a month later. Both times my pregnancy tests came up negative!

Jenny made a doctor's appointment for me because she realized I hadn't had a menstrual period for a while. My boyfriend drove me to the doctor's appointment and waited outside in his baby-blue Cadillac convertible. After the doctor examined me, he asked if I was sexually active. My heart sank because now I had to admit the truth out loud. He confirmed that I was five months pregnant!

On that sunny winter day I told my boyfriend I was pregnant. After the shock wore off, he seemed to be happy. He told me he loved me and offered to marry me. But I wouldn't accept his marriage proposal just because it was the "right" thing to do since I was pregnant. If he had really loved me, he would have proposed earlier.

When I told Jenny about the pregnancy, she said, "I knew it!" Of course, she was very upset with me and concerned about my future. She reminded me over and over, "You made your bed; now you must sleep in it."

I tried to be excited about my relationship with the father of my child, but he began abusing me verbally, emotionally, and physically. When I was seven months pregnant, he pushed me down the stairs. Fortunately, my baby survived.

As the pregnancy started to show during my senior year, the school administrators sent me to a school for pregnant teenagers, which was held in the basement of a Catholic church. We were a small group, but we were all fearful, pregnant teenagers who wondered what on earth we were going to do. The curriculum was easy, and I felt accepted in that small group, as I completed my educational requirements to graduate high school.

Just before graduation in May 1975, I woke up in pain at 2 a.m. I went to the couch to tell Jenny I did not feel right, and she insisted

I call the doctor. My doctor said it was time go to the hospital. I wanted to be the best mother, to represent my child properly, and to look good for his dad; so before I went to the hospital, I put on makeup, blow-dried and curled my hair, and then called my boyfriend to get a ride to the hospital. My labor was painful, and by the time I had my baby, my hair was wet and my makeup was running, but I had made it through. On May 19, 1975, I gave birth to my son, the most beautiful baby I had even seen!

A month after the birth of my son, my high school graduation was approaching. I could hardly believe I made it! When I received my cap and gown just weeks before graduation, I was very proud because I was graduating high school! The day had finally arrived. With anticipation and expectation, my classmates and I dressed in our ceremonial caps and gowns.

People and families were arriving with balloons and flowers at my all-girl high school. I looked around for my sisters (one had graduated a couple years before me and the other was right behind me to graduate) and Jenny. I stretched my neck and opened my eyes wide, but not one person from my family showed up. All my classmates were preoccupied with their families, hugging, kissing, and celebrating. I was alone, watching the expressions of love among others and wondering in my pain why no one showed up for me and why I had to be alone on this special day.

Another special day took place shortly after graduation. I was eighteen years old when Germaine made arrangements for me to meet with my biological mother, Rosemarie, at the food court in Woolworth's. I will never forget how she looked that day—just like Cher. The atmosphere of hurt and loss was almost unbearable as we looked at each other and searched for words to speak. I wanted time to stop, but Rosemarie had to leave. I will never know why she had only thirty minutes, but I was thankful for those precious minutes that seemed to fly by. I did not want our time to end. I needed to know so much more.

If only she knew the love I had in my heart for her; *if only* she knew how I desired to love her; *if only* she knew I had great compassion and forgiveness for her abandonment of my sisters and me! Her leaving that day only amplified my feelings of rejection and worthlessness, but I sensed that she loved me. Over a decade later, when I was in my early thirties (after Rosemarie's death), her sister told me that after our meeting at Woolworth's, my mother kept a picture of me on her kitchen table. The love I sensed from her at our meeting was real.

After graduation, I thought it was time to move out of Jenny's home and move in with the father of my son. However, this meant I would no longer be a ward of the state and I would be cut off from any monetary, medical, or other help.

It did not take long after moving in with the father of my child for the abuse to begin again. It seemed normal to be abused because that was how our relationship progressed. He accused me of cheating on him, even though *he* was cheating on me with a married woman. The accusations and name-calling increased. My life was getting more and more chaotic.

If I asked simple questions like "Where are you going?" or "When will you be home?" he would get angry and say, "Don't worry, it's none of your business." Then he would hit me, take me by the hair and knock my head against the wall, kick me, and spit on me when he was finished. The spit was almost comforting because I knew he was done, at least for a while. I lay on the floor, feeling ashamed and totally responsible for the mess I had gotten myself into just by simply asking those questions. As time passed, the abuse got worse. Many of my friends and family saw my mental and physical condition deteriorating, and believed he might eventually kill me.

I got a job at a local grocery store and often showed up at work crying. Week after week the tears rolled down my face from hurt and hopelessness. The manager of the grocery store where I worked was a kind, gentle man who was attracted to me. He noticed my tears, hurt, and pain, and wanted to help. He told me I was beautiful and that he loved me and wanted to marry me. The violence and abuse at home was escalating, so I finally said yes to the store manager's proposal. I left my boyfriend, and my thirteen-month old son and I moved into the home of my manager's mother until we were married a few months later. Finally, I thought ... a safe place where we would be loved.

Reflections:

As an abused woman, I had no conception of boundaries. I thought I had no rights, and I allowed my thoughts to be manipulated with negative comments like "You're not a good mother. Look at you, you're a delinquent. Do you really think you're a nice woman?"

I had a choice to either try to convince the people I love to see the reality of their misperceptions or outright lies until I went crazy, or to believe the truth about myself that says, "I am a good woman. I am a good mother. I am not crazy. I am not a delinquent." I adopted a saying, "I'm sorry you think that way," and I would walk away knowing I could not control their thoughts.

I came full circle with this principle: *I am not God.* I cannot manipulate or force anyone to think or believe or act a certain way. All I can do is establish boundaries and a fortress of safety for myself.

Are you in an abusive relationship? Have you ever felt frightened or controlled by another person's behavior? There are many things to learn about abusive relationships. Here are a few simple truths you need to know:

- **No one deserves to be abused**—not verbally, emotionally, financially, sexually, or physically! No one … ever!
- **Tell someone!** Abuse is fueled by secrecy. Find someone you trust, and tell your story. If they don't believe you, tell someone else.
- **You are not to blame!** The fault for abuse lies in the heart and mind of the abuser. Don't accept responsibility

for the bad behavior of other persons, no matter how much they accuse and point blame.

- **You are not alone!** There are many people who care about you and will walk beside you through the process of healing. Reach out to other people who are qualified to help. Reach out to God who loves you, who suffers with you, and who will wrap His strong arms around you and give you strength for the journey ahead.

My heart is in anguish within me;
the terrors of death have fallen upon me.
Fear and trembling come upon me,
and horror overwhelms me.
And I say, "Oh that I had wings like a dove!
I would fly away and be at rest;
yes, I would wander far away;
I would lodge in the wilderness;
I would hurry to find a shelter
from the raging wind and tempest."

For it is not an enemy who taunts me—
then I could bear it;
it is not an adversary who deals insolently with me—
then I could hide from him.
But it is you, a man, my equal,
my companion, my familiar friend.

Psalm 54:4–8, 12–13 (ESL)

Bonnie Janet Carol

Germaine Rosemarie

Jenny

Janet 1987

Janet 2007
Living free from abuse for the first time.

Janet Marie and Son Chris 2010

Janet Marie and son Richard 2011

Janet Marie and son Peter 2007

Janet Marie and daughter Tara 2010

Janet Marie's Grandchildren

43

Kenneth Napper and Janet Marie dating in 2008

Janet Marie & Kenneth Napper

Brenda Branson   Janet Marie Napper

Chapter 7

Turmoil, Chaos, and Confusion

Arise, my love, my beautiful one, and come away,
for behold, the winter is past.
Song of Solomon 2:10–11

I WELCOMED THE WARMTH AND relief that my new husband brought to my life. These were very happy days. For the first time ever I was with someone who really loved me. He expressed his love in every way and shared everything he had with me. His family accepted me, and we lived in a nice suburb in New York. I should have been content with this loving relationship and normal lifestyle, but normal was not something I was familiar with.

Within a few weeks, my son's father crossed the state line, looking for me with the intention to convince me to return home with him. When I refused, he threatened to take our son. I called the police, but there was nothing I could do because he had rights as the biological father. Fortunately, he did not follow through with his threat and returned home.

A few months later, I received a letter from him saying he was sorry for all the pain he had caused me. My sister informed me that he was ill in the hospital, and immediately I began to have compassion for him and a desire to nurture him back to health. I felt guilty that my son was not growing up with both of his parents, and wanted desperately to give him a happy home so he wouldn't suffer the painful childhood I had experienced. The wounds of abandonment were still raw and deep, and I wanted to give my son the chance I never had.

This conflicted thinking convinced me to leave my first husband whom I appreciated and loved. For the previous few months he had cared diligently for me and my son, providing for us and protecting us. When I told him I was leaving, he was hurt and confused. Later, he told me I was really messed up and he hated the very sight of me. I felt rejected by the only man who had truly loved me.

When my son's father and I got back together, everything was fine for a few months. Shortly after our reunion and my divorce, we married on Valentine's Day. Soon afterward I was pregnant for the second time and believed I had made the right decision to reconcile with my son's father. I was so happy to be pregnant and excited to see our family grow. After our second child was born, I went back to work, encouraged and hopeful that my relationship was free from abuse.

At home, little red flags were popping up everywhere, even though I pretended everything was okay. My husband accused me of cheating on him. Our home was constantly a party zone, but having his friends around provided a respite from his accusations and mean behavior. He became aggravated easily and often left home without telling me where he was going. The cycle of abuse had begun again, but this time it was much worse than before. Not only did he beat me, kick me, and spit on me during his angry tirades; but one time as his violence escalated he held me captive in our home for a couple of days, literally not letting me out of the house and then demanding that we have sex. When I resisted, he put a rifle in my face, threatened to kill me, tore off my clothes, and raped me. I lay there like a limp rag doll, numb and despondent. When he left the house to buy cigarettes, I realized my only way of escape was to call the police. They came promptly. When he got back from the store, he denied the charges; but it was too late because they had found the rifle and observed my torn clothes. After he was arrested, I never went back to him again.

I was twenty-one years old with two beautiful sons and two failed marriages, trying to make it on my own and pursuing the next available man so I could have a family. By the time I was twenty-three, I had learned to protect myself and take control of my life. I determined that no one would get the best of me anymore, let alone tell me what to do.

After the arrest of my second husband, numerous bad relationships, and two abortions, my first husband invited me for a visit to his new home in Nevada. He had been in contact with my older sister and Jenny, expressing an interest to see me. My family thought it would be best for me to get away from all the abuse I had experienced from my sons' father, so they bought me a ticket to go out West.

This was a very emotional time. In order to escape the craziness of my own actions and the abuse that seemed to follow me, I made the very difficult decision to leave my two baby boys with Jenny. I simply did not have the money to take my sons or care for their needs. It nearly tore me apart, but I was desperate to escape abuse and continue my pursuit of a family, not realizing I was actually leaving the very family I was pursuing.

I made all the necessary arrangements for Jenny to care for my boys and kissed them good-bye. As I boarded the plane for Nevada, I felt like I abandoned my sons just like my parents had abandoned me.

Every time I think of the moments I lost with my boys, it grieves my heart. They missed so much at that crucial growing-up stage because of my neglect, and today I feel they may suffer the effects as grown men who struggle with intimacy in their close relationships.

Upon my arrival at the Las Vegas airport, my first husband met me and within minutes commented that I had put on weight. I weighed 125 pounds. I sensed a very bitter, angry man. I knew something wasn't right, and I was scared, but did not know what to do. I was there on a one-way ticket and knew no one. The kind, loving person I had married was gone. Apparently he had sent for me to get back at me for leaving in the first place. With his affluent Las Vegas lifestyle, he wanted to show me what I had given up. His anger and contempt were more than I could take. He demanded sex. I felt helpless and alone, guilty for leaving him, and afraid of his anger. So I gave in to his demands, only to be tossed aside and treated with contempt and rejection afterwards

I desperately wanted to go home. I felt like I had fallen into a trap! I could not take this type of rejection from someone I thought loved me, and the absence of my children was unbearable. Every time I saw a child close to the age of my children, I fell apart and wept openly, even in public. Day after day, month after month, it was more than I could bear.

When I called Jenny to ask for her help, she told me it wasn't time to come home yet and that I hadn't been gone long enough. Because I trusted her and desired her acceptance, I did not go against her advice; but I felt rejected and everything inside of me told me to go home. In my mind, I had no choice but to find work and get a place to stay. I found a babysitting job during the day for a family with a little boy around the same age as one of my sons. They thought I was a good match, and I felt welcomed.

During the evenings, I hung out in casinos a lot to kill time. In a strange way I felt safe there. It was a place where lots of people were around me; and with a couple of dollars to play the slot machines, I could drink all night. One night I met a young military man who was tall, blond, green-eyed, and very handsome. He had a quiet gentleness and kindness about him. He was stationed at the Air Force base.

We quickly got to know each other by walking, talking, and playing slot machines. Within a couple of months, he asked me to marry him. I told him, "I cannot. I have two children at home, and I must get back to them." I had not seen my boys in five months. He insisted I marry him first and then go get my children. He said if I did not, I might never return. In my heart and mind I knew he was right. I wouldn't return. I was confused and flighty. I also thought this man would make a wonderful father and provider for my two boys. (Sounds familiar?) So I said yes and married him. This was my third marriage, and I was only twenty-three.

His parents sent us a Bible for our wedding gift. He was a little embarrassed, but I remembered as a young person I liked reading my Bible and sensing the love of God. I wanted to encourage my new husband and suggested that we read the Bible together. We read scripture just about every night. My desire to know God as a young child was still real in my heart as a young adult. It felt right and good. I was at peace.

All I could think of was going back home to get my two boys. I promised them that I would be there before school started. I did go home as promised—on their first day of school. I will never forget the joy and pride I felt when I saw my sons walking down the sidewalk. When they saw me, we ran to each other and shared a big hug.

While I was still at home, Jenny's husband died, and my stay was extended. My new husband took leave from the Air Force and flew home to be with me for the funeral. Afterward he returned out West, and I followed within a few weeks.

When I returned with my sons to my new husband, he had become a *born-again Christian*! This upset me. We used to drink and have fun. I had just gotten to the point where I felt I had control of my life, and I could not give up the control to God! When I went with him to his church, I experienced church in a way I had never known before. The people were happy, praising God with uplifted hands, praying, and laying hands on each other; in fact, they laid hands on me. This was very odd and uncomfortable to me.

When I was presented with the Gospel, I just could not let go of my life. Somehow I knew that giving my heart to God then and there was right, but I could not surrender or trust anyone. How could I trust a God I could not see when the very people I could see weren't trustworthy? The wrongful nurturing from my foster father and ex-husbands left me distrustful of surrendering my life to a loving God.

I was so confused. I had moved far away from home with my sons, and now *this* happened! How could I have known this was for my good? Was it? Because I could not say no to these Christian people, I said, "Yes, I will accept the Gospel," but my heart was angry and full of rejection toward God.

With my desire to do things my way and my new third husband's desire to follow God, there was much division in our home. He would not consider divorce, but I could not handle it anymore. I did not have the money to take my boys home, and I needed to get my divorce to leave the state. The hardest thing I ever had to do was call their dad on the East Coast to pick my boys up and take them home. I cried for days and days and days leading up to his arrival. I could not bear to see my little boys leave, so I left the night before their dad picked them up. The very idea—I had just got my sons back, and now my family was gone because of this Christian thing. I feared their father would sow seeds into their little minds that their mother had abandoned them. Worse yet, because of the mess I had created, my boys were being subjected to the same pain and rejection I felt as a child.

In my rebellion and anger I found another boyfriend. This one was a mean, violent man who was also in the Air Force. Eventually, I got my divorce because of my adultery, which gave my third husband a scriptural way out. Because of my decision to say no to God, I struggled for the next thirteen or so years with failed marriages and more physical abuse. I was living in total darkness, ashamed, hurt, lonely. I felt my life was not worth living.

 *Reflections:*

Most abused women know all too well they cannot bear the thought of another person hurting. They want to nurture as they would like to be nurtured. Often they care more about other people than about themselves. Abusers innately seem to sense this inclination and prey on these emotions. If abused women are not aware of this tendency, they will be victimized like I was when I returned to my abusive boyfriend, with the cycle of abuse occurring over and over again.

Some men who are hurt and insecure abuse others. This is not an excuse and does not justify their behavior, but it is a fact that hurting people often hurt other people.

Abuse became my way of surviving at some point. When I was being abused, at least I was getting some attention. This thought pattern had begun with my foster father's abuse and was the lifestyle I had been taught at a very young age. I did not know another way.

Remember my desire to have a family? I never knew until later in life what the Bible says in Hosea 2:16 about the Lord, "You shall call Me, *my Husband*." Since then I have experienced God as my husband. Every time I would go to Him in private, needing the comfort and assurance that I am not alone, He would reveal His presence to me.

When you sense the living God in your presence, there is no want. When we push God aside, we push aside the very essence of what we are looking for in life. If I had known I already had God as the ultimate companion, I wouldn't have gone searching for one.

Instead, as a needy young girl, I went looking for this family man that I longed for.

For divorced women, God is our husband, too. He created everything. He knows what we need, and the amazing thing is when we commit to know Him, we will experience just how beautiful, loving, and faithful He is to us. "Let go and let God" is a motto I have come to live by. Things will happen if we trust in Him. In my need for a man to act as husband and father to me and my children, I wish I had known that Jesus is all those things.

I think the biggest mistake abused women make is to try and make things happen. Having been controlled, we try to control in an attempt to cover up our broken, hurt hearts and spirits. We do this rather than live each day experiencing the God who made us and knows how to love, restore, heal, and make us over if we let him.

Song of Solomon 8:4 says, "Do not awaken love before its time." I learned the hard way that females are extremely emotionally involved when we are sexually involved in relationships. So why do we go kissing, hugging, and touching when we know it will lead to a sexual involvement? Do not awaken love before its time. The time to awaken physical intimacy is after marriage.

One thing I learned about God: His love never fails. I had to come to a place where I realized how much of a mess my life really was and how much I needed God to do for me what I could not do for myself.

Back in my earlier years, I saw God as the man on a cross with nail-pierced hands who died for my sins. But even though I turned my back on him, He did not turn His back on me! He fought for me and pursued me with His love until I said yes!

Dance with me
O lover of my soul
To the song of all songs.
Romance me
O lover of my soul
To the song of all songs.

Behold You have come
Over the hills
Upon the mountains
To me You have run
My beloved
You've captured my heart.[7]

---

7   Lindell Cooley, "Dance with Me," *Encounter with Worship* (Nashville: Music Missions International, 2008), vol. 1, audio CD.

Chapter 8

Running Away

The hunger for love is much more difficult to remove than the hunger for bread.
—*Mother Teresa*

I FINALLY FOUND MY WAY back home and moved in with Jenny. By this time, my boys' father had returned them to Nan's home (their name for Jenny). It was great to see my sons, and they seemed very happy to see me.

But little did I know things were going to get bad again, and quickly. A former abusive boyfriend with bad connections found out I was home, and soon afterward he knocked on the door of Jenny's house, asking to see me. He was mad because I came home without telling him. I have no idea how he even knew about my return. He was persistent in his pursuit, and within weeks after we began dating again, he began yelling and calling me names. When he threatened to put out a cigarette in my hand, I said, "Do it! I don't care." (At that point, I really did not care what he did to me.) So he took my hand and pushed the lit cigarette into my palm until the fire was extinguished. I don't know which hurt the most—the pain from the cigarette or the pain of feeling trapped by abuse.

I was so tired and exhausted from trying to make sense of my life that I wanted to run away. I could not bear the abuse anymore, and I felt like I was of no use to my children. I was living with my foster mother and had no job. I said, "Mom, I can't take this anymore. I need to leave. Please, is it okay? I am so sorry, but I just cannot take it."

With her permission and approval, I booked a standby ticket to visit a friend I had met out West who lived in Florida. As I was waiting at the airport for my flight to depart, my former boyfriend with the bad connections showed up. "Janet, I am so sorry. I love you, babe. Let me get us a house; let's get married. I love you." His empty words of love and kindness, which I had heard many times before, were a smoke screen of lies that promised more abuse. For twenty minutes, he tried to convince me to leave with him, but for once in my life I stood my ground and said no.

When he finally understood I was serious, he yelled at the top of his lungs, "You whore! There you go again, running off and leaving your kids. You are no good. I hate you. You will never be at peace. I will destroy your face—no one will ever want you. I will come and get you and kill you one day." Then he left. For the first time in my life, I felt like I truly did something right by saying no.

Upon arriving in Florida, I stayed with my friend's mom in a beautiful coastline community. Within weeks, I found a job as a cocktail waitress at a beachfront hotel. Life was free and easy, and I had a semblance of peace. But it wasn't long before the same problem that had plagued my life in the past resurfaced again. My "friend" was really the violent, abusive boyfriend I had met out West where I divorced my third husband. Once again, I fell prey to his controlling, abusive behavior.

When I did not do exactly what he wanted, he called me names and lashed out verbally. This "friend" became my enemy as he poured out his unresolved anger on me. What began with verbal abuse, which only wounded me internally and kept his hands clean, escalated into hitting and punching, which exposed his violence when others saw my cuts and bruises.

I felt like a complete failure! How could I have left my children for this? On my way home from work one day, with overwhelming thoughts of hopelessness, I stopped at the beach where I saw an attractive man sitting in a car with his friend, watching the waves. He was dark and handsome. I really wanted to meet him, so I tucked my pack of cigarettes under my car seat and walked over to his car. I knocked on his car window and asked if he had a cigarette. "Yes," he said. "Would you like to come in and smoke some weed?"

I joined him and his friend in the car, and we exchanged phone numbers. Soon we were dating and seeing each other daily. He was Welsh and a surfer, and he lived one block from the beach. We were both in our mid-twenties. For the first time in my life I sought out someone instead of being pursued or pushed into a relationship. I wasn't looking for "kind and gentle" anymore because that gave me heartache, but it turned out that he was very genuinely kind and gentle. We had a beautiful relationship, and he became my fourth husband on March 10, 1985. I was twenty-seven years old.

All relationships have their little quirks here and there, but this time there was no abuse. There was only one problem—his family were drinkers, and it wasn't long before I was drinking every day. Previously, if I had a few drinks a week, that was a lot for me. Now I could drink vodka every day, and if there wasn't juice, I drank vodka and Coke like the rest of the family.

Our beautiful baby girl was born in September. I now had two sons (still living with "Nan") and a new beautiful baby girl whom I had long desired. Life seemed to be going well, except for the custody case my ex-husband filed to gain custody of our sons. He told the authorities I had abandoned them. But in my heart and mind, I left them to spare them from a life of abuse.

I spent many days writing to the judge who had jurisdiction over the custody case in my home state, pleading for my boys, letting him know I had to leave their dad because of abuse, and assuring him I was stable and able to care for them. When I returned from the court date, twelve months after my first letter, I was awarded custody of my children! I was very happy.

Shortly afterward, my two boys (eight and eleven years old) flew to Florida, and I had the family I always wanted. I cherished every moment in the only way I knew how. Dysfunctional living was my only way of life, so I was very self-protective and selfish. I had to have things *my* way. I played God in everyone's life and controlled situations at home and, of course, my children. If they did not do as I asked, there was definitely a price to pay.

When my daughter was two, I became pregnant and gave birth to a beautiful, bright-eyed baby boy, whom we named after his father. Shortly afterward, I went back to the food and beverage industry where I was working my way toward management. I was a people person who got bored often, so this seemed to work for me—lots of people with the scene changing often.

The drinking problem got worse. In almost every photo either my husband or I had a drink in our hands. Though we have many good family memories and our family looked good on the outside, we were not doing well behind the scenes.

The photos of drinking were just a red flag that something was drastically wrong. Drinking led to smoking pot; smoking pot led to pills; pills led to cocaine and eventually to crack. Soon we were selling things in our home and neglecting bills to buy crack. Our love was there, but our life was *out of control.* Although I was able to quit my addiction to drugs, my husband could not. I did the only thing I knew to do—run away, this time to nightclubs.

This was my escape from the reality of my life. I could not take another failed relationship. But as a hurt, lost, and confused woman bored with life, I met a man eight years younger who was carefree and bubbly. Almost every weekend after the children went to bed, I asked my husband to watch after them while I went nightclubbing.

This not only took my mind off my problems, but it took my mind and commitment off my marriage. I did not cheat on my husband but eventually left him because of the cause and effects of his drug usage and my alcoholism. After several years of being separated, I filed for divorce. I will never forget my husband's face and his tears in the courtroom as the session concluded. Within a few years after our divorce, my fourth husband died of an accidental overdose of pills.

Reflections:

Like some of you, dysfunction and abuse were the only things I knew. I was in total darkness, not knowing life *should be* functional and free from abuse. Because of my childhood home environment where men were abusers, womanizers, alcoholics, and full of anger, and because of an early exposure to so many sexually perverse men and women, I lived a life of pain—pain of knowing I was different, pain of not belonging, pain of being lonely, pain of ridicule and abuse. None of this seemed natural, but I thought I was the only one going through it—that no other person on the face of the earth was living this gloomy life even on the sunniest of days.

I knew it was not right to be mistreated or mishandled. But I did not realize there was help for victims of abuse. The hardest thing to do is leave someone you love … or think you love. If I had known about the love of God, I would have had the courage and confidence to get help for myself and my husband. But my usual pattern was to run away from the problem.

Have you heard of "fake it till you make it?" I really never enjoyed smoking weed. The effects left me with no ability to control my choices. While sober I could not say no to much, but while high I was completely helpless. My desire to be accepted led me to "fake it" (doing things I did not want to do) so I could get my needs met.

When people fail to deal with their problems, they either stuff their hurts deep inside where it causes a variety of physical symptoms or they turn to sex, drugs, or alcohol to fill the emptiness inside. When the "high" of romance or addiction wears off, they move on to the next opportunity to find relief from painful memories or circumstances. It's like filling the belly of a starving child with cotton candy—it tastes good for a moment, but the child will eventually die unless they are nourished with healthy food.

Our souls need nourishment just as much as our bodies. Deep soul wounds can only be healed by God's love and through the love of His people. He asks us to stop our random searching for things that fill us up for a moment but leave us empty and wanting more in the end, and He invites us to come to Him for everything our hearts need to be whole and satisfied.

Have you heard the story of the Samaritan woman who met Jesus while she was drawing water from a well? You can read about it in John 6. This woman had five failed marriages and was living with a man at the time she met Jesus. He was probably the first man who spoke gently and respectfully to her ... ever! Unlike other men, He did not want anything from her. Instead, He offered her "living" water—the very life of God to live inside her—to quench her thirst for love and significance forever and ever. Her encounter with Jesus that day changed her life and redefined her as God's beloved daughter instead of the scandalous woman of Samaria.

I don't know what your life has been like or how you have been defined by others because of the choices you've made. But I do know that you are loved and desired by the King of the universe, the Lord of all creation. His invitation to you is not "Come, be good," but "Come, be mine."

Define yourself radically as one beloved by God. God's love for you and his choice of you constitute your worth. Accept that, and let it become the most important thing in your life.

God's love does not depend on you. So please, please, please stop running away when you mess up and run into the arms of the one who totally loves you as you are right now.

I stand anchored now in God before whom I stand naked, this God who tells me, 'You are … my beloved one.[8]

It's hard for me to believe I could be lovely in your eyes,
that I'm really the one You want.

It's hard for me to believe that You would want me
by your side,
that I'm really the one You want.

But You love me, You love me, You love me still.

You love me,
You love me,
and You always will.[9]

---

8   Brennan Manning and Jim Hancock, *Posers, Fakers, and Wannabes: Unmasking the Real You* (Colorado Springs, CO: TH1NK Books, 2003).

9   Todd Agnew, "The One You Want," *How to be Loved* (Memphis: Ardent Records, 2012), audio CD

Chapter 9

Finding God

For I know the plans I have for you, declares the Lord,
Plans for welfare and not for evil, to give you a
future and a hope.
Jeremiah 29:11 (ESV)

ONE DAY I WALKED INTO a photography studio in Florida whose
sign on the door said Hiring. To my surprise I was hired on the spot
(a divine appointment). On my very first day at work, I was invited
to church by an "on fire for God" co-worker who sat next to me. I
thought, *Why not ... what have I got to lose?*

My way of surviving was hard and tiring with minimal outcome.
The end result was the same thing over and over—living with
partners or roommates in between marriages. This was a dead-end
cycle. Individuals who have been abused and neglected know what
I am talking about: we are constantly looking for and needing that
unconditional, constant love and attention that only comes from
God.

I knew God was holy, although I did not know what holy was.
Even without having a relationship with God, I knew *I was not
holy.* In March 1995, I was invited to go to church revival services
described as an extension of the "Toronto Blessing," a world-wide
phenomena of supernatural experiences that started in a church in

Canada. This meant nothing to me, having not been in Christian circles. In fact, to hear someone mention the name *Jesus* was very odd to me. I called those people Jesus freaks in my youth. When I walked through the doors of this church, I saw hundreds of people singing, dancing, waving banners and flags, and loving one another. My first thought was, *these people are crazy*, but my mind flashed back to the little girl who sensed the love of God. Based on that familiar sense, I wanted to understand what was going on. What did I have to lose?

With every passing day of going to this revival, a hunger and thirst was created inside of me that was indescribable. Nothing could satisfy the hunger other than having what was in that church building: God! The joy, peace, expectation, and love were all infectious. I could not get enough, so my two younger children and I went every night.

My heart wanted more and more of God, but I still wondered who He was and whether or not I could trust Him. I rejected God in my twenties, but now I was desperate. As more nights passed, I could not take the desire and tugging on my heart anymore; I had to try God. I had to. My way just wasn't working, and I was numb to everything around me. Could this be my hope? Could I live again?

As I made my way to the altar where many people were praying, it felt right. It felt so, so right. I could hardly breathe. To my surprise, my two youngest children were behind following me. That night I confessed with my mouth, "God, I cannot do this anymore. I confess I am a sinner. I cannot help myself. Please help me. Jesus, come into my heart and show me your way of living." At that moment, I experienced His amazing love and peace. Within weeks, my two children had given their lives to Jesus as well.

After seriously giving my life to God, I sensed a small change and a big desire for more change. How was it possible for a person, *me*, to be in total ruins, having lived a dysfunctional life for over thirty years with no hope of change, yet to experience this tangible peace, joy, and hope for something greater?

Up until that night when I gave my life to God, I'd been pretending in my head that I was something and was capable of getting anything I needed. I hadn't known the real truth up to this point that I *was* someone—a person created by God who loved me with an everlasting love—and that I had value, purpose, and hope.

Shortly after becoming a Christian, I sensed God saying to me, "Janet, there are a lot of things happening here (at the church revival), but some are not of me and have distracted you from me. Look for me ... hear me ... keep focused and you will find me."

I just could not believe something so profound could come into my thinking like that, yet I knew it was God. After that, I did not let others' experiences or emotional responses during the revival services distract me.

# *Reflections:*

God never gives up on us! He is always near, drawing us to Himself. It is up to us to respond. Why wait to start your new life when you can live in His bounty and provision now?

I waited to give God my life until I was absolutely at the bottom and desperate. The good news for desperate people is that God is faithful. He's still waiting for you. You don't have to get to a desperate place to turn your life over to God. Do it now! Why wait until you're thirty, forty, fifty, sixty, seventy years old or more to enjoy life?

Matthew 10:39 says, "He who finds his life shall lose it. And he who loses his life for My sake shall find it." Now I am giving my life to God and living a new life with joy, hope, expectation, and victory over my past! God has a plan for your life and a hope for your future if only you will trust Him. "You will seek me and find me, when you seek me with all your heart, I will be found by you, declares the Lord" (Jeremiah 29:13–14 ESV).

Laying flat upon my back,
All the world in motion,
Everything goes by so fast,
I feel like I'm frozen.

After all is said and done,
Did I fail to mention
Everything I haven't done,
All my good intentions.

This is my holy hour, this is my world on fire,
This is my desperate play, this is where I am saved.

Let my ruins become the ground You build upon,
Let my ruins become the start.
Let my ruins become the ground You build it on
From what's left of my broken heart.[10]

---

10   Bebo Norman and Jason Ingram, "Ruins," *Bebo Norman* (Seattle: BEC
Recordings, 2008), audio CD.

Chapter 10

The Counterfeit

*I don't have a clue why God loves me. But I believe
in the core of my being that He does.
So I surrender to it. I stop fighting it. I cease trying
to figure it out. I collapse on it.*
—*Nicole Johnson*

I BEGAN ATTENDING CHURCH REGULARLY and joined a Bible study group. Even though I was identified as lost, lonely, and hurt, for the first time in my life I was around people who cared for me. Through my study of the Bible, I learned who I was, what I had, and what I could be.

My Bible study group consisted of mature, godly women who loved on me and my two youngest children. Their love was nurturing, caring, and sincere. Because I could not take another rejection, the only way I could cope with their love was to believe they really did not love me for myself but only because they loved God. But after six months of their constant, unconditional love, I finally realized these women chose to love me. That was when my healing process began.

Since the girlfriend I was living with had no interest in God, my Bible study group encouraged me to apply for an apartment through the Salvation Army where rent was based on income. The application deadline was approaching, so if I was going to apply, I had to swallow my pride and do it. I desperately wanted to trust God, and since these people seemed to be filled with His love, I applied for the apartment.

Through the prayers of the people God put in my life, I got the apartment! I was in shock but so very happy. When the good news came that I was awarded the apartment over all the other applicants, I was humbled, embarrassed, and excited all at once.

Shortly afterward, my roommate asked me to go to the bar with her. I did not want to go but could not say no to her, because I wanted her to like me. She kept pleading with me to go with her so she wouldn't be alone, so I did. As I sat in the bar, I purposed in my heart to be good. I had only one beer, and I kept my focus on the football game. When the game was over, I went to the corner and sat in a chair near the pool tables where I thought I would be safe. After a few moments, a good-looking man came up to me and asked me if I would play pool with him. I said no.

Before the night was over, my girlfriend was playing pool with him, so I went over and joined in on the conversation. This man offered me a drink, and I said yes. Even while we were sitting at the bar drinking, I could not contain my joy of receiving Jesus into my heart and the new life I was feeling and experiencing, so I told him all about it. I could not believe what came out of this man's mouth. He said he knew God, and not only that, he knew the Bible!

He offered his number to me at the end of the night, knowing I was going to be moving soon. I took it because I thought I could use his help when I moved, but I also was amazed and interested in the God he knew.

When the Salvation Army apartment was available, my new church friends helped me paint, fix up, and pray over my new apartment. They helped me start a new life. I was so weak that I could not do it without the love and care they provided.

I was proud of my little place I had with my youngest son and daughter. My daughter and I shared a bedroom, and my youngest son had his own room. My children, especially my daughter, were very excited about the new apartment. This was the very first time my daughter and I had the chance to bond. I had neglected giving her my affections because of the hurt caused by my mother's abandonment of me when I was two years old. Because of my deep-seated resentment toward my mother, I did not have healthy relationships with my daughter or any other female.

As I leaned on God, trusted Him, and experienced His unconditional love, I began to be healed of that loss and pain. With God's help, I was also able to forgive myself for my shortcomings as a mother and to love my daughter more intimately. I was able to love her with the love of God first and then with my own mother's love for this beautiful daughter of mine. What a joy! Today we have a healthy, loving, mother–daughter relationship.

I made a commitment to God and did not want another man in my life—only God. Then one day that good-looking, Bible-talking man I met at the bar called me. How was I to handle the situation with this man who was obviously interested in me? This good-looking man knew the Bible backward and forward, and he had charisma too. I wondered if this was the man I prayed for all those years ago, before I asked God into my heart.

In my early thirties, I prayed the only way a Catholic woman knew how. (Remember, I went to the Catholic church, and although I called myself a Christian, I did not follow God.) I got on my knees, folded my hands, bowed my head, and prayed to my heavenly Father: "God, will you please give me a man, one who loves you with all his heart, one who would know all my flaws but love me just as

I am, one who loves me just as you intended?" This time my prayer was sincere and from my heart rather than a repetitious one to keep from going to hell. When I got up, I experienced a peace I had never felt before—a peace so calm and assuring that without knowing anything about faith, I knew "that prayer" would be answered.

The guy from the bar and I got together on several occasions. I was excited to invite him to my Bible study, and my Bible study friends wanted to meet him. He told me he was not in church and was backslidden; therefore, he wasn't ready to go back to any church or Bible study group. I had absolutely no idea what "backslidden" meant, so I said, "Okay, it's all right." When I told my Bible study group why my friend would not come, they warned me to beware of "wolves in sheep's clothing." Even though I was a little uneasy in making further contact with this man, I ignored the discernment God was trying to give me through my new church friends ... wishing and longing for the one man whom I had prayed for.

We eventually became a couple. Shortly thereafter, he started pressuring me to move out of the Salvation Army apartment God had given to me and my children. He reasoned, "There are people out there who have no place to live, and those homeless families could have your apartment. You now have a place with me." I did not have the courage to say no to this man, and rationalized I would be helping someone else to have a place to live, so I left my apartment and moved in with him.

Three months later he asked me to marry him. I don't know why I said yes, other than I thought he was the one God had for me. He said he knew God, and he knew the Bible. I thought, *Wow, a Christian marriage!* I sensed he was lonely and had many hurts from his past, and I believed I could love him back to health.

Trying to follow God was not easy in this relationship. As he continued to pressure me to move in with him, I decided not to fight it anymore and gave in. The pressure to have sex increased once I lived with him. It would have been so much easier if I had just said no from the very start, but I did not have the strength to say no to this man after I had already promised I would marry him. When I told a pastor at our church, he offered for me and my two youngest children to move in with him and his family, which we did.

With all that love, all the support, and all the counsel, I still wasn't strong enough in God to stand by myself. I chose to keep this man in my life, and the pull of his seducing spirit eventually had its way. I was told by my husband-to-be, "It's time to come home," so after spending a few weeks with the pastor's family, I returned home.

Within six months we were married. Three days before the wedding, I knew with everything in me and by the sound of my heart pumping that I was *not* to marry this man. But this people-pleasing, dysfunctional lady could not say no. We were married in December 1995. It was a day I wish had never happened. I married this man because my flesh was stronger than my spirit.

This marriage was by far the most abusive. Within the first few days of our marriage, my new husband was sleeping on the couch. Within a month, I had a black eye and bruised ribs because He thought I was unfaithful. I will never forget him sitting on me, slapping and hitting my face while punching my ribs as though I was a rabid dog. I was emotionally, mentally, and spiritually sick with all the bad decisions I had made, and in my irrational state of mind I felt sorry for him because he hurt me! Two weeks after being beat up, I was lying on the couch coughing in pain because my ribs were still tender. My husband became aggravated and told me to get over it.

Not long afterward, as I was walking to the bank to make a ten-dollar withdrawal, I heard a truck screech its tires in the middle of the road. I turned my head to see what was up, and there was my husband getting out of his truck, mad as could be, and accusing me of being a streetwalker. He took me by my hair, literally pulled me into the truck, and slammed the door shut.

The incidents got worse and worse. The electricity was shut off in our home because he wasn't working much and wouldn't allow me to work. Because I was a new Christian and did not know the Bible, I thought I had to listen to everything my husband told me. You know the verse "Wives, obey your husbands." When I failed to obey, he told me I wasn't a Christian woman. This was my life in 1996: washing dishes with our neighbor's garden hose in the yard because I had no lights in my kitchen and it was dark.

Out of deep desperation to get away from the hurt of rejection, withholding of finances, and verbal abuse, I went to the bathroom and slid down the wall to the floor. I thought about taking pills so I could end my life of desperation, but I did not have the courage to go through with it. Today, I am glad I did not.

I was terribly confused. I had given my life to God in hopes of a new life but ignored all the obvious signs warning me about this man. He claimed to be a Christian but pressured me to have sex outside of marriage. He was physically and verbally abusive, accusing and blaming me, calling me names, making me crazy, and cruelly saying he should have left me in the streets like my mother had all those years ago.

With all the issues in our marriage, we made an appointment with our pastor for counseling. My husband was clever and charming in the counseling session as he told one lie after another. I was crushed and hurt that the pastoral staff believed him. In one of the meetings, my pastor yelled at me, "You're a liar!" Although I did not go back for further counseling with my pastor, I stayed in my marriage and continued going to church.

Later I sought professional counseling. My counselor told me the next time I was battered, I had the choice either to do nothing and get beat over and over again or to contact the local authorities and have them handle the situation, which would probably have meant jail time for my husband. When I was physically attacked again, I decided to follow the advice of my counselor and reported the abuse to the police. He tried to deny the charges, but the police took him away. It was comforting for me to discover that the police are fully aware of the characteristics of abusive men.

Within a week, I was at the police station canceling my charges as most abused women do. Afterward, my husband never physically hurt me again, but he made up for it by putting his face as close to mine as possible, nose to nose, and screaming as loudly as he could, "I could slap you right now," or "I should kill you."

I know I could have left this man, but I felt I had to keep the commitment I had made before God when I married him. I thought things would get better if I could just be a better wife and that maybe it was my fault when he hit me or yelled at me. But things did not get better, and my despair deepened; so I turned to God for help.

I was invited to a women's tea at church. The tables were set beautifully. Worship dancers came in dancing before God to beautiful music. I was sitting in the back near the door. I became overwhelmed at the beauty of His presence. My mind told me I was too dirty, not good enough to be in God's presence. I could hardly contain my tears, and when I could not take it any longer, I slipped out the backdoor and went into the bathroom where I slid down the side of a stall and wept uncontrollably.

A few minutes later, a lady came to check on me. When she saw my condition, she sat on the floor with me, hugging me, loving me, and explaining to me that God didn't see my past but only the newness of my life in Jesus. I had no idea God loved me just the way I was. He knew everything about me, and still He chose to love me right there. I had been trying to do everything right so He would love me. I did not know about grace.

Here I was, trying to please God at every turn; but the more I tried to please God with my works, the angrier I got with myself for not measuring up. I felt defeated and came to a point when I said, "No more, I cannot do this Christian thing." Trying to look good, act good, seek God, go to church with all the lovely ladies around, so pure while I was not—I just could not do it anymore. This was the first time I heard the voice of God in my heart and mind say, "Good, now I can do for you what you cannot do for yourself." Wow! Was that God telling me I do not have to please Him, that He is already pleased with me?

"Therefore if anyone is in Christ, he is a new creature; the old things passed away; behold, new things have come" (2 Corinthians 5:17 NASB). This verse finally went from my head to my heart. As I was lying on the couch, thinking of God and my life, this thought occurred to me: I am a new person. The old Janet had passed away (died), and I was born again. I wept and wept at the thought that Janet, the girl no one loved, the girl people took advantage of, the girl who wanted all of God, had died. The spiritual death of my old nature was so real that I was gasping for air. It was so sad to me ... after all it was *me*!

Within moments I went from sobbing to laughter because I had just realized that I really, really, really had a new lease on life. If the old nature is dead and I am still alive, I truly am a new creation and have a new start on life! I no longer had to be condemned about my past and all the wrong things I did. If I felt guilty or ashamed of my past, I was reminded, "Hey, that person is dead." I may still have to walk out of old habits and old thoughts, but with God's help I can do it!

Reflections:

Because I was new to the whole Christian thing and very dysfunctional, the mere fact that a man spoke about Jesus to me was like hitting the jackpot for a woman looking for a Christian man. Here are some very important things I learned:

1. **Never go looking for a man.** After a broken relationship, take a year or more spending time getting to know God and being satisfied with His love as you heal emotionally and spiritually. The more you learn about God, the more you will recognize godly characteristics in other people, especially the man you want for a husband.

2. **Just because somebody claims to know Jesus and can quote the Bible does not mean that person is walking in the love of God.** The Bible says that even the demons know God and can quote scripture. Beware of people who like to talk about God or take pride in going to church, but who don't really know God and reflect his character.

3. **When considering a marriage proposal, listen to godly counsel.** The book of Proverbs talks about victory and safety when we seek godly counsel. I did not listen to the people God put in my life through the local church who warned me of wolves in sheep's clothing. I ignored the very signs that would have kept me from such great pain, and suffered the consequences of my decision to marry outside God's will.

4. **Listen to the still small voice within you.** If you ask God for wisdom, He will give it to you, but you must

be willing to listen to His voice and not follow your emotional pull.

5. **Beware of quick proposals from strangers.** Abusers like to take advantage of vulnerable women who are looking for love. Paul warned about this:

> For among them are those who enter into households and captivate weak women weighed down with sins, led on by various impulses, always learning and never being able to come to the knowledge of the truth. (2 Timothy 3:6–7 NASB)

That was me in a nutshell. I was a woman weak with sin, wanting to know God, but yet led by various impulses—impulses to find affirmation from men, help from men, love from men, comfort in drinking, comfort in sex, comfort in talking and shopping, and the list goes on.

6. **Parents, I implore you to look your children in the eyes, tell them you love them, and above all, show them you love them.** My heart aches sometimes at the knowledge that I can never get those years back when all four of my children were young and so needy of my love. I thought of others with no regard for my needs or, worse yet, the needs of my children. Being spiritually unstable causes you to put a man you hardly know before your children. Spiritually unstable women do all kinds of things they don't want to do and regret, but have no power in and of themselves to do otherwise.

7. **Find a counselor who has experience with abusive relationships.** Abusers are very slick and come across as charming people who have it all together. Unless you counsel with someone who knows the characteristics of an abuser, you may not be fully understood and even be

considered a liar or a lunatic. Many pastors and church leaders are well-meaning but often are not trained in the dynamics of abuse.

8. **God understands what you are going through, and He will be with you.** God was there all the time when I was young, waiting to help me overcome the hurts and wrongs that had been done to me and the hurts and wrongs I inflicted upon myself. He knew me in my mother's womb, and he saw me when I rejected Him. When I did not feel His love anymore, it was because I had left Him. He never left me.

Maybe you have said to the Lord, "Do you know what a broken woman I am? What in the world can you do with a woman like me?" I have prayed those prayers to God for so many years. It seems like some would want you to believe God can't use broken people. I'm here to testify that God stoops down in His great, great mercy and tenderly raises up every woman who lays her broken life on the altar of His glory.

One thing I want you to keep in mind, in the hardest times, when it seems like everything is falling apart and you're going down holding all the pieces, is that there is always a hidden work of God. When you think that God is distant or that maybe even God has turned against you, I want you to remember that in the unseen, God is plotting for your joy. He is planning the redemption of your brokenness.[11]

---

11   Angela Thomas, *Do You Know Who I Am? And Other Brave Questions Women Ask* (New York: Howard Books, 2010).

Chapter 11

God Will Make a Way

*I will restore to you the years that the swarming
locust has eaten.
Joel 2:25 (ESV)*

THIS IS THE TRUTH THAT changed my life: I am truly born again, *a new person* with a new slate and a new name. I stood firmly on this truth and used it to battle negative thoughts of who I used to be and of accusations in my mind that I would never change. The more I studied my Bible and prayed, the more I became aware of a deeper, more intimate relationship with God. As I began to listen with an open heart, I sensed His direction for my daily living. As I took each baby step to follow God instead of my normal pattern of running away, I experienced His faithfulness and care even in the small details of life.

Even though my husband still treated me badly, I had hope that our marriage would get better. During one of our arguments, I walked out the back door and sat on the porch, just to get away from his rudeness. I thought about staying there for a while; but the thought came to me that if I stayed away, the devil wins, but if I press into love, without violence, God wins. I got up and walked into the house. Somehow the words I needed to say came out of my mouth to diffuse the situation, and all was well for the rest of that evening.

The strategy my husband used of being nice just to get his own way no longer had its intended effects on me. The "honeymoon" phase in our cycle of abuse became a point of reference rather than a prediction of false hope.

Finally, after volunteering at several charities, the day came when I had my husband's permission to work. My paychecks were used to pay the bills, and my husband spent his paychecks on whatever he wanted. During the next three years, I had found and lost four jobs. My husband's constant phone calls and my own distractions caused me to get fired. I could hold on to my job with the sympathy of my employer for a couple of months, but not beyond the ninety-day probation period, because in the end I was not their problem.

I became known at church as a "real" Christian woman in spite of what my husband would say. When a friend asked me if I wanted to interview for a ministry position, I said yes! This job changed my life. The founder of the Christian 12 Step Ministry was the first authentic Christian man I had daily contact with. He was like a father to me and knew without my saying anything that my marriage had problems. My husband was still calling me, stopping by, and making situations uncomfortable for me. Although my boss had great empathy for my situation, and even though I was a very good worker, I was let go after seventeen months because of lack of funding.

Within two months, I had another job in a Christian ministry, where I stayed for more than three years, working my way up to marketing director. Here, God showed me what real Christian men were like. After several years of seeing consistent kindness, patience, gentleness, and long-suffering on a daily basis, I came to realize that Christianity was more than habit, but an actual way of life or lifestyle.

The acceptance and education I received from my two bosses in their efforts to help me see my worth and value is one of the primary reasons I can love people today. Here, God shaped my character through the pain and rejection I felt from fellow workers, but this time the rejection was nothing more than a difference of personalities. Thirty years of experiencing abuse in one form or another distorted my thinking so that when people did not agree with me, I felt they were rejecting me. God helped me understand that this was not true. I now appreciate honest friends, and even if they do not agree with me, I know I am still accepted and loved.

At home the verbal, emotional, and financial abuse continued. Now in our seventh year of marriage, I finally learned that what my abuser was doing to me was the same thing he would have done to another woman if I hadn't been around. It was *his* character causing the abuse, and it did not matter whom he was married to. This took such a weight off my shoulders because finally I could stop blaming myself. The pain and sting of his actions lessened until they had minimal effect, and I was no longer bound by the abuse. Taking away the personal aspect of it helped take away the sting. Although I hated what he was doing, I learned to love the man God had created.

After enduring this dead-end marriage for so long, with no hope for unity, I filed for a divorce. Four weeks later, my Christian boss extended an invitation to my husband and me to go to a marriage conference. Although in my heart I was so mad at the invitation because I finally had the courage to get a divorce, I smiled deceivingly and said, "Oh great, thank you so much."

I learned two things at the marriage conference. First, it takes *both* the husband and the wife to be in a personal relationship with

Jesus Christ as their first love, then loving each other, to have the marriage God intended.

Second, God is the one who makes a way of escape, not I. After the marriage conference, I felt I had filed for divorce without considering God's timing and purpose, so I went to the courthouse and withdrew my divorce application. Two months later, my daughter told me my husband was trying to pick up her boss. Surprised and a bit leery, I called this woman and she confirmed the story, adding that he also stayed with her friend for two days until she found out he was married.

Now that I had evidence of his unfaithfulness, and scriptural grounds for divorce due to adultery, I went to the courthouse the next morning only to find out they had never closed my original case. I was spared the extra expense of refiling, and it wasn't long before we were divorced. I have had perfect peace since then.

Once again, I was a single mom, working and providing for my children, now ages fifteen and seventeen. After dragging them to shelters throughout the course of my abusive marriage, I finally began to understand the importance of healthy boundaries and the sobering responsibility of applying them. The best time of my life was the year I had with my teenagers after my marriage was over. This gave me quality time with them. All of my children have suffered the effects of abuse because of my life choices. These were years that can never be replaced, but the disrespect and mistrust in our relationships are in the process of healing and restoration. Thanks be to God.

Reflections:

My personal relationship with Jesus continues to grow deeper and deeper. His loving presence and peace is something I crave, just as when I was a child. But now I know I don't have to do anything except seek Him, and He will always be there.

What about you? Are you still trapped in the cycle of abuse, trying desperately to find a way of escape, looking for someone who will know you deeply and love you passionately? Then perhaps you should stop looking for another man to fill that job because the perfect man does not exist in your world today. Jesus is the only one who can satisfy the deepest longings of your heart.

My friend, Debra Moore, wrote these words for you, dear reader. Sit down, put your feet up, and drink deep from these truths:

If you are looking for a man who will love you, no matter what …

If you are looking for man who will make you his first concern when you open your eyes each morning …

If you are looking for a man who will protect you from all dangers …

If you are looking for a man who will watch over you while you sleep …

If you are looking for a man who will believe in you at all times …

If you are looking for a man who will always trust you …

If you are looking for a man who will comfort you when you are sad …

If you are looking for a man who will provide for all of your needs ...

If you are looking for a man who will sacrifice his life for yours ...

If you are looking for a man who will think of you all day long ...

If you are looking for a man who will smile when he hears you call his name ...

If you are looking for a man who will never let you down ...

If you are looking for a man who will always see the beauty in you ...

If you are looking for a man who will never hurt you ...

If you are looking for a man who will wait for you when you leave him ...

If you are looking for a man who will never neglect you ...

If you are looking for a man who will always be the same, yesterday, today, and tomorrow ...

If you are looking for a man who will be whatever you need, whenever you need it ...

If you are looking for a man who will never lie to you ...

If you are looking for a man who will hold you in his love while you sleep ...

If you are looking for a man who will listen for your first waking breath ...

If you are looking for a man who will always forgive you when you make a mistake ...

If you are looking for a man who will stand by your side when others abandon you ...

If you are looking for a man who will wipe away all of your tears ...

If you are looking for a man who will be your strength when you are weak ...

If you are looking for a man who will always speak a good word on your behalf ...

If you are looking for a man who will look for ways to bless you each day ...

If you are looking for a man who will take away all of your fears ...

If you are looking for a man who will be all you need all the time ...

I know that man:

He is my father, God.

He is my savior, Jesus Christ.

He is my comforter, the Holy Spirit

No person can ever love you like this. This is impossible for mere man.

No human being has the power to be all of this all of the time, only God.

It is unfair for us to tell ourselves as women that we deserve to be loved this way by a man because what you are actually looking for is divine love.

It is an unreasonable expectation to do so.

If any man tells you that he can love you this way, he is a trickster.

It is also unreasonable for us to think that we can love a man in return like this.

If we do this, we are tricking ourselves and setting ourselves up for abuse.

It is even more unreasonable to allow someone to convince you that you should be able to love them like only God can.

Understand that people have faults; divine love is faultless.

There is no love like his. He can make your childhood pains and memories disappear.

He will give you the strength to forgive the unforgiveable.

He will heal your soul wounds.

He will take away the evil words spoken over your life.

He will give you peace, love, acceptance, contentment, and safety.

He is divine love![12]

---

12   Debra Moore, "If You Are Looking For a Man ..." used by permission.

Chapter 12

Redemption: God's Best!

You have taken up my cause, O Lord; you have
redeemed my life.
Lamentations 3:58 (ESV)

SOUTH AFRICA WAS CALLING MY name. I had some friends in South Africa and worked in Florida with South Africans as a board member for a local teenage pregnancy home. I really wanted to travel to South Africa, but a year and six months passed before I had peace to go. In the meantime, my friends from South Africa traveled to the United States for ministry training and stopped to visit me. This was a precious family consisting of the father, mother, daughter, son-in-law, and grandchildren. Before they left, they said, "Janet, if you ever come to our country, we have a bed and breakfast where you can be our guest." After fasting and praying, I felt confirmation that God was calling me to go to South Africa. The second confirmation I received when a missionary from South Africa I had never met before walked into the mission office where I was working. He connected me with his travel agent who gave me a special "missionary rate" to travel overseas and a case of Bibles to distribute in the country.

In October 2006, I traveled to South Africa. Three weeks seemed like three days. Just before I left South Africa, my friends' pastor asked me to prayerfully consider coming back to help them establish a home for abused women. I immediately went to my room, knelt by the bed, asked God if this was something He wanted me to do. God reminded me what he had brought me through, and of the years of ministry preparing me for such a time as this. I felt like I had my answer and said, "Yes, Lord, I will do this for you." The peace of God flooded my heart with the grace to move forward. In March 2007, I returned to South Africa in obedience to and service for the Lord.

After my year's work was done and I came home from South Africa in March 2008, my friend and mentor, Catherine Kroeger, founder of PASCH, encouraged me to start a ministry for abused woman here in the United States. One night I decided to pray, "God, do you want me to start a ministry for abused women? If so, I need to have a name when I awake. Otherwise I'll let this go." I fell soundly asleep and woke up the next morning to the name "GOGirl." At first I had forgotten about my prayer but then realized, *Wow, I have to do this work! Wow, my God has spoken to me!* Today, Global GOGirl has an international board of women who are passionate about sharing God's truth to help women overcome abuse God's way.[13]

After five years of being single and totally content, and after saying no to marriage proposals from three men during that time, I finally met the man I had prayed for as a young adult. We were married on January 16, 2009. The words spoken to me by the ladies in my first Bible study group had become my foundation: "Janet, why do you want to settle for good when God wants to give you His best?" God's faithfulness with each baby step I took so many years

---

13   See http://globalgogirl.org.

ago led the way to this point in my life. I knew if I did things God's way, I would be all right.

Kenneth Napper is my best friend and husband for life—the man I always desired. He is not only handsome but also godly. He unconditionally cares for, nurtures, and supports me in every way. He prays for me daily and for the ministry of Global GOGirl.

Together we are one; together we live for Christ.

 *Reflections:*

If you have experienced any form of abuse, this book was written for you. It is my heart's desire that you see yourself in my story and acknowledge that you are not alone. My prayer is that you find the courage to try Jesus Christ, who is watching over you right now, gently saying, "I love you. Follow me."

I don't know what your situation is, how many times and ways you've tried and failed to find love and purpose in life, or what depths of despair you have suffered. You may be sitting in a mansion or in a jail cell; your struggle with addiction to drugs, alcohol, food, or sex may be overwhelming; you may even be perched on the brink of sanity, just trying to hold on one more day. Whatever place you find yourself in today, there is hope for you. There is someone who knows you, who hears you, and who loves you. His name is Jesus. No strings attached. No need to clean up your act before you come or to prove that you're good enough. His invitation is simply, "Come … be mine."

Arise, my love, my beautiful one, and come away,
for behold, the winter is past.
Song of Solomon 2:10–11

If you're still hesitating, let me tell you the story about a woman in Luke 7. Her life was completely messed up; but when she met Jesus, everything changed. His love transformed her and made her beautiful and clean. She wanted to do something to show Jesus how much she loved him. Here's the rest of the story:

A woman who had lived a sinful life brought an alabaster jar and broke it at the feet of Jesus. I am certain it was the most beautiful thing she owned. It represented her very life. At His feet, she poured out all her longings, all her struggles, all her attempts to measure up, all her manipulations to try to get love. She poured it all out at the feet of the One who could love her completely. She finally found the right feet. And Jesus was moved ... He recognized in her a heart of longing. He knew the sinful attempts that she had made to meet them apart from God. He forgave her.

And He will forgive us. We, too, have brought the alabaster jar of who we are to the wrong feet. We have tried to get love from others by using beauty. We have brought our pain to people who could not ease it, though we hoped they could. There is only one set of feet that can heal us. The ones with the holes.[14]

---

14   Nicole Johnson, *Fresh-Brewed Life: A Stirring Invitation to Wake Up Your Soul* (Nashville: Thomas Nelson, 1999) Google eBook (my italics).

CONCLUSION

This is my story ... from rags to riches. May God use all the good and bad aspects of my journey to give you hope and encouragement as you travel your own road. Learn from my mistakes and celebrate with me all the things God has done. I bow before Him with all the love and gratitude this heart can hold, and say thank you.

Rags

The orphan I was. The abuse we experience.

Riches

Blessed *is* the man [or woman] who finds wisdom, and the man [or woman] who gets understanding. For the profit from it *is* better than the gain from silver, and its produce more than fine gold; she *is* more precious than rubies; and all the things you can desire are not to be compared with her. (Proverbs 3:13–15 MKJV)

Abuse

But realize this, in the last days difficult times will come. For men will be lovers of self, lovers of money, boastful, arrogant, revilers, disobedient to parents, ungrateful, unholy, unloving, irreconcilable, malicious gossips , without self-control, brutal, haters of good, treacherous, reckless, conceited, lovers of pleasure rather than lovers of God holding to a form of godliness although they have denied its power; *Avoid such men as these. For among them are those who enter into household and captivate weak women weighed down with sins, led on by various impulses, always learning and never able to come to the knowledge of the truth.*

(2 Timothy 3:1–7, my italics)

National Domestic Violence Hotline: 800-799-SAFE
International Directory of Domestic Violence Agencies: http://www.hotpeachpages.net/index.html.

How To Become A Christian

1. **Realize you are a sinner. Sin separates you from God.**

   "You see, all have sinned, and all their futile attempts to reach God in His glory fail." Romans 3:23 (The Voice Bible)

   "Sin is more than just wrong choices, bad decisions, and willful acts of disobedience that violate God's Word and are contrary to His will. It is that and much more. Sin is missing the mark or deliberately stepping over the line. Like an addiction, sin takes hold of us and causes us to act in ways we never wanted." --The Voice Bible, page 1376

2. **Know that God loves you so much He sent His only son, Jesus Christ, to pay the full price of your sins through His death on the cross and resurrection from the dead.**

   "God sent His only Son into the world so that we could find true life through Him. This is the embodiment of true love, not that we have loved God first, but that He loved us and sent His unique Son on a special mission to become an atoning sacrifice for our sins." 1 John 4:9-10 (The Voice Bible)

3. *Ask* God to forgive you of your sins.
   Believe that Jesus Christ paid for your sins on the cross.
   Confess that He is Lord.
   Receive God's gift of eternal life!

> "So if you believe deep in your heart that God raised
> Jesus from the pit of death and if you voice your
> allegiance by confessing the truth that Jesus is Lord,
> then you will be saved! Belief begins in the heart,
> and leads to a life that's right with God; confession
> departs from our lips and brings eternal salvation."
> Romans 10:9-10 (The Voice Bible)

> "If anyone unites with our confession that Jesus is
> God's own Son, then God truly lives in that person
> and that person lives in God. We have experienced
> and we have entrusted our lives to the love of God
> in us." 1 John 4:15-16 (The Voice Bible)

"Dear Lord, I know I am a sinner. Please forgive me. I believe Jesus died on the cross for my sins and rose from the dead. I trust Him with my whole heart, and accept His invitation to be my Savior and Lord. Thank you for your love and promise of eternal life. Amen."

If you have become a Christian or rededicated your life to Christ today, please let us know at *globalgogirl@gmail.com* or Global Gogirl, 7700 Getwell Road, Southaven MS 38672.

Janet Marie Napper is founder and director of Global GOGirl and Global GOGirl South Africa, as well as a volunteer chaplain. She is married, with six children and eight grandchildren.

Janet is available to speak at churches, women's retreats, and women's conferences on the topic of abuse.

To host a teacher's certification training in your area on "Overcoming Abuse God's Way," or to start a support group in your area for abused women, contact Janet by e-mail at globalgogirl@gmail.com or by phone at (901) 605-8087.

Brenda Branson is founder and director of Broken People, a non-profit organization offering resources, encouragement, and hope to people who are hurting, coauthor of *Violence Among Us: Ministry to Families in Crisis* (Judson Press), and author of four training manuals and many educational articles on domestic violence as well as over a thousand articles on faith-based topics. She has been a guest on the *Focus on the Family* radio broadcast, on Moody Broadcasting Network, and on the *Harvest Show* and *Time for Hope* television programs, addressing the issue of abuse.

Brenda is available to speak at churches, women's retreats, and women's conferences on topics including "A Woman's Journey with

God," "Love Stories—Real People Encountering a Real God," as well as seminars on relationship issues and domestic violence. Contact her at (270) 871-7812, by e-mail at *bren1756@yahoo.com*, or by regular mail at P.O. Box 323, Hanson, KY 42413.

Visit *http://brokenpeople.org* and *http://facebook.com/brokenpeople* for free resources and encouragement for hurting people.

CPSIA information can be obtained at www.ICGtesting.com
Printed in the USA
LVOW07s0041300915

456246LV00001BA/22/P